Fire Your

Financial Planner

Who to Fire,
Who to Hire—
and Why

Ron Firmin

MASTER SERVICES PRESS

This book is dedicated to my dear father,
Famous Joseph Firmin,
a simple man whose love for life
and trust in God made him a great man.
I can only aspire to imitate his
loving and gentle spirit.

Contents

Foreword

Are you a baby boomer who is serious about taking control of your financial future, but not quite sure how to get started? If so, you hold in your hands a book containing both a heart-warming personal story and a financial game plan that makes sense.

Ron Firmin is a man with a modest formal education who made and lost small fortunes on several occasions. This book is not about a (financial) fairy tale life with a (financial) fairy tale ending. Instead, you will learn about real-life experiences—something you can relate to—and how a truly remarkable man demonstrates astonishing faith and determination. You see, Ron Firmin's life story is still a work in progress.

Irrespective of the circumstances, many Americans have inadequate plans for retirement. On top of that, unexpected setbacks occur for all of us. As a great philosopher once said, "Most people don't plan to fail, they fail to plan." Nowhere does this quote ring more true than in personal financial planning. Most people simply wait until it is too late.

Getting started is the key. *Fire Your Financial Planner!* provides the basic tools for developing a personal financial plan. In just over 125 pages, Ron shares his experience in raising himself from a very humble childhood in Louisiana to owning a large construction company and holding millions of dollars for retirement. He was set. He was living the American dream. And then, after taking on one, final project to cap his career, he lost it all. Not part of it ... all of it! The story of how Ron made it back again to financial success, including lessons he learned along the way, is what separates *Fire Your Financial Planner!* from other books on retirement planning.

In a series of twenty-one lessons, Ron explains what he learned on the way up, on the way down, and back up again. In Lesson 2, for example, he explains how to make the most of your assets, how to limit your spending, and suggests that the 401(k) system will fail many baby boomers. He also provides information on what can be done to compensate for this failure. Lesson 10 explains the rationale for equity investments in the stock market. In Lesson 16, he covers one of the most important concepts in the book: the Rule of 72. Lesson 17 discusses how your home mortgage can be a powerful wealth-building tool.

Above all else, *Fire Your Financial Planner!* is honest. It's the honest story of a man who was described by his father as having escaped poverty … three times! The text meanders through a maze of personal stories and real-life adventures, but ultimately shakes you to the core with simple truths. A candid, in-depth discussion with yourself regarding your financial situation is a difficult and unfamiliar task for most people. To make it easier, Ron's personal life story makes it vivid and real, including fantastic business success, being cheated by a customer, losing his job, launching an entirely new career, and developing high performing teams of people … while simultaneously delivering on his commitment to being a devoted father, a loving husband, a loyal son, and good neighbor.

Ron Firmin shares the feelings many people experience, but are hesitant to admit. Based on these experiences, the lessons contained in *Fire Your Financial Planner!* inspire an authentic perspective that is critical to success. Facing such brutal personal facts head-on is the key to unleashing the true motivation required to make changes in life.

So go for it! Take the first step toward planning your financial future. I think you will find *Fire Your Financial Planner!* is both a heart-warming story and a sound plan for charting a more secure retirement for you and your family.

Joe Herring
Chairman and CEO
Covance Inc.
Princeton, New Jersey

Acknowledgements

Whatever degree of grace may be associated with this text is due to the ever watchful and always caring eye of my wife and first-line editor, Sharon. She has never wavered in her support for this project.

My son, Jeffrey Skye, lived this story with us. Throughout the writing process Jeff has been dependable and supportive. He reminded me these same lessons apply to young adults. Jeff and his wife, Andrea, and my granddaughters, Skyler and Kristin, inspired me to continue writing.

My dear brother, Glenn, died during the completion of this manuscript. His investment experience and our frequent discussions helped to make this a better book for the average investor. I will always be grateful for his help as a brother and fellow baby boomer. Glenn passed away at the age of fifty-eight on May 18, 2007.

For his guidance and incisive criticisms, I wish to thank my mentor, and fellow author, Terry Price. His suggestions and encouragement as I sought my writer's voice have always been inspiring.

Many thanks go to my personal financial planner and principal of Secure Financial Group, Frank "Bucky" Minter. Bucky has never failed as a resource and a confidant. His experienced eye has helped me shape my suggestions, balancing them with the changing facts affecting the financial industry.

My life as a writer really changed when I met my editor, Jamie Chavez. Jamie and I swiftly found that we were of like mind and filled with curiosity about the world around us. After our first wide-ranging discussion, I knew she was the right person for the job. Jamie understood what I wanted to accomplish and with her help I believe that we have a book that you will refer to not just once, but over and over again. Thank you, Jamie!

Through this process I have been blessed to have some of the finest CPAs, business leaders, and financial planners review my manuscript. For their kind comments and direction I am most grateful. They have given me increased confidence that the baby boom generation will embrace and identify with my experiences.

Many baby boomers have had a hand in shaping the dialogue for the next twenty years. I am privileged to have known and learned from some of the best of them. I wish to thank all baby boomers who have touched my life and have contributed to our growing understanding of how to best manage and control our financial resources.

Author's Note

Fluctuations in economic markets have been a constant feature of the US and global economies. There are many factors over the last ten years that seem to have accelerated trends, particularly technological advances in communications and the vast expanse and accessibility of the Internet.

From time to time, monumental shifts occur in various industries. Of course, the media feeds upon and chases the sensational and the catastrophic. That truth in no way diminishes the tremendous negative impact that developments may have on the American economy. The global markets may also be adversely affected.

For example, historically, the US home mortgage industry has been one of the major underlying pillars of financial strength of this country. We have to acknowledge that even with fluctuations in this sector, the long-term prognosis has to be that there will continue to be growth. As our children, grandchildren, and succeeding generations enter their earning years, they, too, will require housing and mortgages. The home mortgage industry is not going away. I suppose we could say that the entire US financial system would have to fail for that to happen.

The home mortgage industry has always had periods of growth interspersed with periods of consolidation—the industry has mirrored the real estate industry. We are familiar with the real estate terms *buyer's market* and *seller's market*. In the home mortgage industry, seasonal adjustments are commonly called *purchase market* or *refinance market*. Such adjustments or changes in the kinds of home mortgages closed are easily tracked, and there is considerable information available on mortgage association and banking Web sites to substantiate those assertions.

Over the past fifteen to twenty years, there have been many product introductions that have allowed options to informed consumers. This fact alone dictates that consumers have a personal responsibility to be well informed. The banking industry has been responsible for creating and introducing a variety of mortgage products, all of which have had the scrutiny and approval of state banking and mortgage industry agencies. Many of these are the same products that banks so roundly disdain in the media as being detrimental to the consumer. They have failed to educate consumers—therefore, they say that the uninformed consumer is incapable of making wise choices regarding mortgage options. For millions of competent baby boomers, that smacks of the same elitist pap that we have been fed all of our lives by the powers that be.

The banking industry has done a poor job of educating or making options available to the average consumer that *put more money into the hands of home mortgage holders* rather than the banks themselves. Why would any bank tell you how you can make more money and they can make less? Consequently, over the years, as the needs and wishes of consumers have grown, the banks lost more and more of their mortgage clients. A few years ago they began to realize that when a consumer had a home mortgage with a bank, the consumer would typically stay with that bank and purchase other bank products, including savings and checking accounts, investment accounts, and so on.

With respect to home mortgages, the fact is the banks have proved to be incapable of successfully reaching out and providing consumers the kind of service that they have benefited from for nearly two decades. The banking culture and the ingrained paradigms that mandate their actions suggest that consumers will find new and better ways to manage their home mortgage. It is likely that revolutionary concepts which fill that hunger will come from entrepreneurial concepts – not from banks.

It is impossible for any book to be absolutely current with respect to fluctuations and trends. The information provided on mortgages will be to empower you with a basic understanding of the industry and some of the major events affecting all consumers. You will also learn about the various kinds of mortgages so that you can make a better evaluation of what works best for your circumstance. Just knowing the basic language of the home mortgage industry may save you thousands of dollars. And there are some little known facts and options available that you will be glad to discover.

Since no industry or economic market is immune to the tug of many and often opposing forces, it is imperative that individual investors remain informed by staying personally involved in the management and direction of their own personal retirement accounts. This is true whether or not you have a financial planner.

Introduction
But Wait, I Haven't Boomed Yet!

When I was forty-one years old, I lost more than three million dollars—everything I had. I was looking at my future rushing at me like a freight train, with absolutely nothing financially to show from all the years I'd worked in the past. Through the preceding years there were many little lessons that I had learned, but I was so caught up in the moment that I did not take time to reflect seriously on them. I was even blessed with wonderful spiritual mentors and the best of parents, yet I failed to identify a trusted financial mentor.

There are basic financial lessons that are timeless. However, without some wise direction, you are pretty much left to trial and error. You may have learned that a penny saved is a penny earned. But if you don't understand how money works, that may not mean much.

Learning from the experiences of others can save you a tremendous amount of heartache. It is my hope that as you uncover and understand the substance of the lessons that follow, you will be moved to become more involved in managing your own financial affairs. The little lessons contained herein will provide the key to unlocking the door to relative financial security.

* * *

So what if you have no savings, no investments, and, like me, you are a baby boomer approaching retirement? In truth, a very high percentage of boomers have set very little aside for retirement.

Forbes magazine tells us that most people born between 1946 and 1964 are probably behind in accumulating a nest egg that will last them for even twenty or so years of retirement.[1] This means, on the one hand, that you're in good company. On the other hand, and more importantly, it means the time left to create any kind of personal retirement account (PRA) is reduced. The time available for the Rule of 72 (see Appendix B) to work on your behalf is severely diminished. What do you do?

First, assess what your actual financial situation is today. You must honestly review all of your assets and all your liabilities. You may be surprised when you do such an evaluation. You may find that you *do* have assets that, if properly put to work, could provide you some measure of ongoing income in the years to come.

A number of books, including Mitch Anthony's *The New Retirementality*[2] have excellent charts that may be used for the purpose of such an evaluation. A competent financial planner or even your insurance agent will likely have a program that could be helpful and these are usually available at no charge. (A caution: you are trying to gather information. You are not ready to buy any product at this point.) Or you can turn to Appendix A for a worksheet I've developed that will help you get started.

While there are many Web sites that may help you evaluate your personal financial situation, there is one in particular that I wish to call to your attention. The reason this one is so good is because it allows you to look at virtually every area of potential investment. It will allow you to explore and better understand how various options work considering your personal circumstance. Check it out at www.financialcalculators.com/ConsumerCalcs.htm.

If you have, for example, $50,000, you can experiment with ways of dividing the money among savings certificates of deposit, stocks, and rental property, or any other combination. It is good to experiment with a variety of scenarios. This will help you to understand what options may be best for you. It will also make you more knowledgeable as you speak with your financial advisor and convey to him your wishes. While he advises and executes on your behalf, you should remain in control of your PRA.

Second, make sure you have an emergency fund. If you don't already have a rainy day account to care for unexpected expenses like dental work or any type of insurance deductibles, you'll want to establish one now. Experts have varying opinions as to how much you should have in this emergency fund, but it should be in an interest-bearing account that remains liquid at all times. I have seen recommendations from a minimum of six weeks of income to six months of income for an emergency fund. Different circumstances dictate what you view as adequate. Here is one place where a competent financial planner can be a help. Having your emergency fund in place will allow you the freedom to consider alternative investment strategies that involve a little more risk.

Third, determine whether there is some recurring income available to put into a savings instrument or investment vehicle. At this point, it is not the amount that you set aside. It is just critical that you begin to set aside something. If you already have some savings, it is important that you seek to increase the amount dedicated to that purpose. You notice I used the word dedicated. That means that you absolutely do not use it for any other purpose than for savings.

Later we'll discuss some alternative investment strategies that allow you to purchase stock yourself for as little as $10 per transaction. Again, it is not the amount that is important. It is critical to get something going. As one very respected stock market authority says, it does not matter how much cargo you have on your ship, you have to get it out of the harbor.[3] In other words, historically the stock market has moved upward, although there have been declines from time to time. But if you follow all the charts, it is clear that the market, over the long haul, trends upward. So this option should not be avoided simply because you currently have no investments or your available funds for investing may be small. With the advent of the Internet, the market is available to small investors like it never has been in history. That may be the greatest story of the success behind the stock market in recent times.

There is something else to keep in mind when considering investing in the stock market. The goals of a fifty-five-year-old will be different than those of a seventy-five-year-old. The former stands a good chance of benefiting from a long-term investment strategy whereas the latter is likely to need his funds over a shorter period of time. As you know, if the market takes a dip it can take a few years to fully recover—so if your goals are short-term, the market is much more risky.

Finally, view managing your savings, investments and retirement as part of your job description. Now that you have started to save and to invest, the next thing you must master is consistency. Remember, if someone asks you what you do, confidently answer that you are a carpenter and that you manage a retirement fund. If you are a truck driver, you also are a money manager. If you are a housewife, you are also an investment strategist.

Does this mean that your whole life will be absorbed with managing your retirement? Where will you find the time?

Let me ask you this question. Do you have a garden? Do you grow flowers? If so, do you regret the time you spent in the spring cultivating the garden or planting the flowers? Do you feel that it was not part of your job description? Or do you look to the benefit of your efforts? Do you look forward to seeing the garden grow? Do you look forward to harvesting the fruits of your efforts? Do you look forward to the delightful, fragrant flowers when they're in full bloom?

What is my point? The point is once you have begun to turn your attention to your PRA, spend some time every week monitoring your progress. It may be as little as thirty minutes per week. Wouldn't you spend that much time weeding your garden if you really wanted it to be productive? Why should you spend any less time on your PRA? Some people spend a little time every day. You control your own schedule. Be consistent about two things: reviewing your PRA weekly and making regular savings or investment contributions.

This does not mean that you necessarily make portfolio changes weekly. What it does suggest is that by staying informed you will begin to anticipate trends in the marketplace. You will begin to understand the movement of money and all of this will make the management of your PRA much more productive.

Part of your new job description is making sure that you access the best and most reliable help as you determine your unique needs. The good news is that you have plenty of choices when it comes to working with a financial professional. However, before you start calling or asking for referrals, you should do what I've suggested earlier in this chapter: you have to thoroughly assess your financial situation, goals, and needs. You should also address the benefits you expect to obtain from working with a financial professional. Your answers can point you in the right direction.

For example, some financial professionals will work with you to identify your life goals, develop and implement an investment plan, and provide ongoing advice. There are others whose job is to assist you with very specific concerns, such as choosing the most advantageous savings plan, purchasing a long-term insurance policy, or developing a retirement savings plan for your small business. Once you decide what it is that you need help with, you will be ready to interview a potential financial planner.

In my case, I chose a financial planner with whom I had developed a friendship over a period of time and our relationship has grown into one of mutual trust. As I often say, "I trust Bucky with my wallet and my wife!" It would be hard to say more about the integrity of someone you trust to give you good financial advice. When my needs require some additional help, I am comfortable in having my chosen financial professional refer someone to me. Then I take it upon myself to do my homework and be sure that person is a good fit for what I need.

Financial professionals charge for services in numerous ways. Before engaging one, be sure you understand how he or she gets paid, and make sure it matches the way you want to pay. Here are some ways that financial professionals are compensated:

- A percentage of the value of the assets they manage for you
- An hourly fee for the time they spend working for you
- A fixed or retainer fee
- A commission on the products they sell
- Some combination of the above

There are potential benefits and possible drawbacks in each compensation method. The determining factor is your needs. When you have your information arranged and your questions written out, you'll be ready to locate a financial planner that can best help you achieve your goal of a worry-free retirement.

Listed below are some of the different financial professionals that you may need to call on as you begin to grow and protect your PRA. You can also access some excellent information and search for qualified financial planners online at the National Association of Personal Financial Planners Web site, www.NAFPA.com.

Financial Planners
These professionals generally take a broad view of your financial affairs and function in the role of your personal chief investment officer.

Investment Advisors
As the title implies, investment advisors focus more specifically on managing your investments. In some cases investment advisors are also financial planners. Most of them provide you with investment advice and are compensated on an annual basis by a percentage of the assets they manage for you. Investment advisors generally fall into one of two categories: those who offer this advice to individuals or businesses, or those who offer advice and asset management as well (often for corporate clients, hedge funds, and/or mutual funds).

Registered Investment Advisors
In the United States, a financial advisor should be registered (with the SEC or with the state in which the firm does business) depending on the dollar value of the assets that receive continuous and regular supervisory or management oversight by the advisor. In order to be registered with the SEC, a firm must have more than $25 million under advisement.

Stockbrokers
Stockbrokers are intermediaries between buyers and sellers of stocks and bonds and are compensated by commissions made on the buying and selling.

Insurance Agents
Insurance agents help you with your insurance needs, from property and casualty to life insurance and annuities. They can help you with health insurance and long-term care options, as well as offer risk management strategies.

CPA/Accountants
A CPA is a professional licensed by a state to offer a variety of accounting services such as simple tax preparation, financial audits, business evaluations, and succession planning for small businesses.

Estate Planning Attorneys
These lawyers focus on estate needs and can draft your will, durable powers of attorney, and health care proxies. In addition to creating trusts so your assets can pass directly to your beneficiaries without going through probate, estate planning attorneys can develop strategies that enable your favorite charities to make the most of your gifts. (My financial planner helped me engage a competent estate planning attorney to care for these matters. Since the attorney provides services to all the financial planners with this firm, there was not only beneficial savings that resulted but also superior service.)

* * *

There is one more thing that I would like to sincerely recommend. If you are married, get your spouse involved and be sure that the two of you share a common idea of what your needs and goals are. This will make the effort that much more enjoyable and productive.

So—you are a boomer who hasn't boomed yet. Don't despair! Maybe nobody told you that you needed to be the steward of your own money. Nobody told you that your job description included being a financial planner. Now that you know what your job is—go do it. Get busy and become the best financial planner in your family. Who knows what may open up to you. It may be the start of something really big. You may begin to develop that most elusive of all dreams—hope for a retirement that you can shape as you would *like* instead of being driven solely by outside forces.

One thing you must realize is that not everyone will appreciate your new resolve. In fact, it is likely that some will think you are "going through a phase." They will humor you and listen knowingly when you tell them about some of the principles that you have reinforced in your life. But you know better. This is the point at which you are going to make a real change in your life. You will reach out for this new job description realizing that you have the most to gain from your PRA provided you manage it wisely.

Congratulations! You are hired! How much can you earn as the manager of your own PRA? How much do you want to be paid? What are you worth as a financial planner and manager of your PRA? The income derived from such efforts will vary but one thing is certain. You will be paid commensurate with your efforts.

* * *

The lessons I have to share with you cost me more than three million dollars, but they don't need to cost *you* that much. And the information that follows is only an example of the kinds of sources and strategies available. This does not represent an endorsement. It is rather a good start as you continue your research. It is not necessary to examine every single alternative that may be available. As you continue your education and growth as a PRA manager, you will quickly dismiss many ideas that do not measure up to your needs and desires. You will develop your own risk versus reward measurements. The decisions you make will be your own!

Now, to understand the lessons in this book, I need to tell you a little about my humble beginnings.

The Baby Boomer
Generation Arrives

I *remember waking up at 3:30 a.m., anxious and excited about putting on my new outfit and cowboy hat, gloves too. I was now nine, almost ten years old. Today at 6:00 a.m. my father would deliver my brother and me out to the cotton fields for our first day of picking cotton. What an adventure! You see, my grandfather thought it would be good if we could say later in life that we had that experience.*

Born amidst the cotton and cane fields of central Louisiana, we did not know the difference between wealth and poverty. All we knew was a loving home, good Southern cooking, a caring mother, and kind father. A typical day after school would find us playing baseball in the lot next to our house, climbing trees, exploring the woods nearby and, during season, catching crawfish. We didn't have a cane field, but when the fully loaded cane trucks drove slowly past our house, we would run behind one and grab a long stalk sticking out and just hold tight as the truck pulled away. The drivers always knew we did that and I believe they chuckled because they understood the old Biblical principle of gleaning. You cannot imagine how sweet it is to chew a stalk of sugar cane just cut from the field.

So out to the cotton fields we went, as though we were going off on an exploration. It didn't take long to realize this was hard work. An average worker in the fields routinely picked in excess of 150

1

pounds of cotton in a day, dragged his shoulder bag out to the truck, had it weighed, and collected his earnings for the day. How humbled we were to learn that first day that we could not come close to keeping up with experienced pickers.

I vividly recall one little black woman in particular who was a paragon of efficiency and effectiveness. She picked cotton as though it were the grandest occupation with the most purpose ever. When, after days of hard work, I finally picked a hundred pounds, I could hardly believe it when I watched her bag get weighed. She had worked side by side with me all day, neither of us stopping— but she had picked over two hundred pounds. When I looked back at rows we worked, I could easily see the difference. My side was white with remaining balls of cotton; hers was picked clean.

LESSON 1: Any job worth doing is worth doing well.

This lesson pays off doubly well with respect to managing our finances. Our generation has so often been caught up with new things, gadgets, and even recreation that we have not taken time to do a good job when it comes to managing money.

We would never think of building a house with no foundation. We know that garments with no lining do not have the usable life of one with a superbly sewn lining. Would you consider driving your car for tens of thousands of miles without changing the oil?

No. So what makes you believe that you will have resources available to you in a year, five years, or ten years if you don't do a good job *today*? Many act as though they can achieve a relatively worry-free retirement without doing a good job of managing their finances. You recognize that such a thought is absurd, yet, as a generation, the evidence is clear that we have not done a good job.

There is a great lesson in all of this. Dad always told us, "If someone hires you to dig a ditch, don't be satisfied unless it is the best ditch possible, with straight sides, cleaned out and deep enough to accomplish its purpose." Or as the Bible puts it in Colossians 3:23, when you are doing a good job, don't do it as though it's just for men, but as though it is for God.

The days of my youth during the mid-1950s and early 1960s were filled with wonder and a quiet sense of security. As far as we were concerned, the word stress had not yet been invented. While my maternal grandfather had experienced success in business in the early twentieth century, the great Louisiana flood of 1927 virtually wiped him out. He was able to retain his home, the adjoining properties and a small country store that provided for his growing family of nine children, including my mother, the second youngest. It was a comfortable home with a porch that went all around the house.

What fun it is to remember those days when we went to visit MaMe and PaPe. You could hear MaMe and Mom inside cooking while we played in the yard under the watchful eye of my PaPe and Dad rocking on the porch as they discussed world events.

My paternal grandparents had always been farmers until PawPaw worked in the slaughterhouse during the last years before he retired. They subsisted on very small Social Security checks, the truck garden at the rear of the house, and the help of their two daughters and Dad. MawMaw and PawPaw were such humble, sweet people but also gave us a sense of strength, devotion to truth, love for God's word, and above all, kindness.

LESSON 2: Make the most of your assets.

My grandparents made the most of their meager assets. They planted, tended, and harvested their own garden. And then instead of watching television (they didn't have one), they would spend time canning their fruits and vegetables so that they were available during the winter season. Even though they did not have much money, they made wise use of what they had available.

The idea of being frugal does not appeal to many today. The hype of the advertising world heightens our desire for more things. But what do you believe you truthfully require each day to care for your needs without depriving yourself? It is so easy for us to be molded into thinking that the usefulness of an appliance, an article of clothing, or even an automobile is only until the next model or style comes out. There is much that we can utilize without appearing old-fashioned.

For example: more important than the style is that an article of clothing be clean, comfortable, and fit reasonably well. What is the real purpose of an automobile? Isn't it transportation? Isn't it to get you from point A to point B?

The advertising world has taught us a culture of consumption and waste. We live in a throw-away society. Manufactured goods come with planned obsolescence.

If you really wish for your money to work harder, consider this. When buying goods, products or services, do you think of the real life cycle costs of your purchase? Or do you just look at the upfront cost? The life cycle costs represents the real cost of your purchase over a period of time. Doesn't it make sense to insure that, provided there are options, you should purchase items that are more durable, will last longer and maintain a style that will still be acceptable after multiple seasons? Over time, purchasing quality goods may prove to be the least expensive choice.

A wise person recognizes that his assets are not just spendable dollars, but all the other things we may possess that have some value. Making good use of your assets just makes sense. And it makes you money. You can begin to quickly add value to your PRA as you realize savings driven by a wise use of your assets.

You can also make the most of your current assets by taking advantage of whatever free money may be available. I am not suggesting that you become a latter-day Jesse James—but there are opportunities to obtain free money that are so easy it feels like stealing. There are a number of ways of accumulating free money. For example:

Limit your spending! This is so obvious that it can be overlooked but the reason I've put this recommendation at the top of the list is because it's something everyone can do. We have already admitted that we baby boomers have wanted to have all the material things available, and we have bought into the marketing madness that, like it or not, governs our lives. But we can stop.

As a society, the American consumer has become the Pac-Man of global consumption. The children of baby boomers are surpassing even our unquenchable thirst for consumption. We must convey to our children, some of whom are in their late twenties or early thirties, the benefits of availing themselves of free money. Just think of how comfortable their retirements might be if they start sooner than we have (and don't forget the Rule of 72)!

Does this mean depriving ourselves of basic needs? No—but then it is not our *needs* that are the cause of our problems. It is our desire for more and better things—and the fact that we want them now. Changing our outlook on spending can avail us of free money, that is, money that would have gone to the bottom line of some company we don't even own an interest in. For this suggestion to make any sense, it is very important that you create a budget and understand where your money is coming from—and where it is going. When you identify how you can limit your spending, then you'll find funds are freed up for sensible investing for the future.

Matching 401(k) monies. If you have a 401(k) through your employer, you should seek to maximize the matching funds your company puts into the account. This is free money in two ways: first, it reduces your IRS taxes, freeing up more funds for your PRA, and second, the matching funds are company money *over and above your salary* and not subject to immediate taxation.

On the other hand, be realistic and cautious about your 401(k) investments. If you have or wish to start a 401(k) investment, it is worth being informed about certain problems with the system. A variety of sources, including MSN Money in an article titled "How the 401(k) system fails most people," have warned of problems with 401(k) investments.[4] In this article the author, Scott Burns, quotes Brooks Hamilton, a benefits attorney and computer geek, who describes in detail how fewer than 5 percent of workers who rely on their 401(k)s can expect to retire in dignity. He asks a couple of very compelling questions: "If only 5 percent of the people can retire in dignity, can the board of directors, the investment committee, the trustees, the accountants, and all the providers claim they've honored their fiduciary duty?" and "If a general took an army of 1,000 into battle and returned with 50 survivors, leaving the rest as casualties on the field, what do you think would happen?"

At best, 401(k) plans can be only part of the solution for a well-diversified PRA. They should be entered into with caution and with full understanding. Very few understand the challenges and the pitfalls of 401(k)s. You should make time to become informed. In a CNN Money article dated July 9, 2001, it was stated that "the average account in the popular 401(k) retirement savings plan lost money last year for the first time in the plan's 20-year history despite thousands of dollars of new contributions." Remember the MSN Money article by Scott Burns, "How the 401(k) system fails most people." Clearly, there are problems that you need to recognize as you weigh the relative value of a 401(k) as part of your PRA. Have your financial planner or advisor carefully explain available options.

If you are a small business owner, you should look into a Simple IRA plan, which allows similar opportunities to the 401(k) above.

For the 1099 income individuals, several insurance companies, such as Sentry Insurance Company, have excellent plans that allow you to maximize contributions into your PRA with great tax advantages.

Speak to your property and casualty insurance agent to find out what you can do to lower your premiums. He can give you a list of things you can do to reduce premiums. – For example, perhaps you already have a security and alarm system in place or have recently decided to invest in one. Have you advised your insurance agent to determine if that will result in a lower premium?

My agent is one of my old school buddies. John Slaughter has enjoyed a distinguished career with State Farm. He points to a number of additional ways that policyholders can save money on insurance—in effect creating free money. John says, "Raising deductibles, unless you have extremely large deductibles, won't save you enough to justify them. I feel the best deductible on your homeowner's policy is $1,000. On your cars, the $100 on comprehensive and the $500 on collision are, in my opinion, the most cost-effective deductibles."

With State Farm, you reduce your premium if you attend and complete the 55ALIVE program taught by AARP. Other insurance companies may have similar programs. The AARP program is chock-full of tips that may save you from serious injury in an auto accident. Seniors traditionally feel they are safer using the back roads and keeping off interstates—yet statistics show that most of their accidents occur at intersections on secondary roads. Parking lots are another place where many senior accidents occur.

This is important because of safety, obviously, but also because fewer accidents translate to reduced rates. If you go ten years without having a loss claim, your insurance premium may be reduced. Ask your company if you qualify for a reduction in premium. While you are at it, find out what other ways your insurance company has to create free money.

The largest amount of free money available to most consumers can be found in **reducing or eliminating credit card debt**. If you can reduce or eliminate interest payments on credit card debt, it translates into found money. It makes no sense to have $10,000 in a bank drawing 1–2 percent APR while at the same time paying 18–21 percent (or more!) on a $10,000 credit card debt. Every competent financial authority will advise you to reduce or eliminate credit card debt.

Postponing some of your desires can free up money for investing or savings. Just changing the look and feel of your vacation may put money in your pocket. If you have a week off, why not consider three or four days' vacation away instead of the entire week. Spend some of the time around home doing maintenance or lawn work that you would ordinarily pay someone else to do. For some, this one action could free up $1,000 or more per year.

Never drive if you can walk. For the majority of us, a walk of a mile or less would not be a problem with just a little conditioning. Keep a record of how many trips of one to two miles you make in the course of a month. You may be very surprised. Why drive three-quarters of a mile to a drive-through for burgers and then wait, with car idling, for your sandwich? Are the savings worth it in this day of increasing fuel costs? Think of the health benefits from walking that mile-and-a-half round trip. I won't even get into what the burger does to you but at least you could offset the calories to some extent. Need I mention bicycling?

Just think about what it would mean to the environment if every baby boomer reduced his or her gas consumption. What if you slowed down and took the time to enjoy the trees and flowers in your neighborhood? Why, the cost of fossil fuels might even go down—resulting in more free money! You might even get to know your neighbors, who might then be inclined to join you. Pretty soon whole neighborhoods might get into the act.

How about just bundling short trips together? How many times do members of the family go for short drives to the grocery, dry cleaner, or bank? Would it be meaningful if you reduced your gas consumption by one or two tanks per month? In times past, perhaps, this did not have the merit it does today. But in this day of escalating fuel costs, the savings could amount to $400 to $500 or more per year. As the manager of your PRA, would you like another $40 to $50 per month of contribution? I would think so. See Appendix B for some tips for better fuel economy.

Make your used stuff work for you. Remember that old adage, one man's trash is another man's treasure. Have you thought of going through your attic or basement and separating out items that you have not used in a year or more and don't need? At one time or another we've all fallen victim to some catchy advertising and purchased something that we've used very little, or never. Perhaps you should think of them as assets—free money—if you just sold them.

One financial planner I know who recommended this course of action to a client says the client raised several thousand dollars by selling off items, some of which had not been used in over three years. For example, the client still had a riding mower in storage, although he was now living in a condominium. He sold the riding mower for over $2,500, and eliminated a $40 per month storage bill.

If you sell some unneeded household items, then wisely move the majority of those funds into your PRA, you have suddenly increased your contributions and your potential for earning interest income. And think of the space you will have created in your attic and basement!

Don't forget big ticket items that you once placed great value on but no longer utilize for one reason or another. I am talking about boats, motor homes, motorcycles, vacation timeshares, and many other items that you may come up with. Upon thoughtful reflection, you may choose to begin using some of these items again. But if you don't think that you will be using them over the next year, or if their use is very limited, you may want to seriously consider converting them to cash. How often have you heard it said, "My two happiest days as a boat owner were the day I bought my boat and the day I sold it"? That boat owner invested the money he realized from the sale of his boat into his PRA, of course!

There are numerous other things you can do to access what might be viewed as free money. Here are a few other areas that you may have overlooked.

In the area of health insurance, there are a number of things you can do to maintain manageable costs. A proper diet, along with improved eating habits and exercise, may result in a decrease in blood pressure. Aside from the many health benefits (and reduced spending on doctors and drugs), it could result in a reduction of life insurance premiums as well. When I worked for the bank, there was a program that tested employees' fitness. The nurse set reasonable targets for weight, cholesterol levels, and percentages for body fat. As those targets were met, the employee moved to the next level, which resulted in a considerable reduction in health insurance premiums. In this program employees were tested each six months, so there was a continued monitoring of progress.

Even if you are not employed by a company that has such a program, doesn't it make sense to institute one yourself? Working with your personal physician, set up a maintenance program that will keep you healthy and fit for life. What a healthy way to free up money!

A wonderful way to free up money for other purposes is to **have a plan for charitable giving**. The US tax code allows taxpayers opportunity to be philanthropic in large or small ways during their lifetime and realize a tax benefit in so doing. Estate planning opens up additional opportunities to free up your money for not only your beneficiaries but also for causes that you identify as worthy of support. My friend Terry Price, a respected financial planner and author puts it this way: "Seek to bless others as you have been blessed." Be sure to speak to your financial planner and/or tax attorney about how you can free up monies in this way.

You could keep working. In 2000 the US Senate voted 100 to 0 and the House of Representatives voted 422 to 0 to repeal the earnings limit for seniors aged 64 to 69. This action will provide seniors with incentive to continue working and being productive. Before the former law was repealed, retirees had to forfeit one of every three dollars earned above $17,000 per year. My father and father-in-law would have really liked this law in the years after their retirement. They could hardly see the benefit of continuing to work under the old law.

Yes, a powerful way to find free money is to avoid wasting what you have, and to make the most of it. You can change your financial picture by just looking for ways to save money.

And perhaps some of these suggestions are not for you. But maybe they have given you some ideas about how you might access free money. Now, get a sheet of paper and see if you can think of some other ways to free up money. Get your spouse and family into the act. At first they may think you're crazy, but if they understand your purpose and your goal, they, too, may get into the act. They may begin to learn that this can be fun. They may come to the realization that this effort can reduce pressure and stress. As you watch the fruits of your efforts begin to grow, you will feel that whatever effort expended was worth it. After all, it is *your* PRA that we are talking about and you are the financial planner and the manager.

* * *

My father had only completed third grade when he began to work to help support his family before the war. At sixteen he was able to get into President Roosevelt's Civilian Conservation Corps (CCC) and was sent to California to help fight forest fires and build roads through the sequoia forests.

His pay was a little over $100 per month. He kept just enough to obtain some necessities, sending the remainder home to Louisiana to help his parents and sister Dorothy. To this day, Aunt Dot remembers Dad's work and assistance with loving appreciation. Aunt Dot and Uncle Buddy, like Dad, passed along this same work ethic, willingness to share with others, and integrity to their children and grandchildren.

LESSON 3: Sometimes sacrifices have to be made.

Making sacrifices means that we are willing to voluntarily postpone some of our desires. Responsibility may require that other things are more important than the immediate and temporary pleasures of life. The willingness to choose to pursue other important goals while foregoing personal desires is the very definition of sacrifice.

Some individuals make sacrifices because they are dedicated to a cause or a mission. The fulfilling of such a mission can become the touchstone of our life. Later, upon reflection, we may find that it was not such a sacrifice after all. It can even make life more rewarding to know that we can be happy no matter what circumstance confronts us.

When we accept the sacrifices that must be made to reach a particular goal, we may see that we gain a measure of calmness. We learn endurance, patience, and become emotionally and spiritually stronger as a result.

Now think about this from the standpoint of your PRA. When we sacrifice some of our material desires and postpone purchases so that we can fund our PRA, how do you think you will feel five, ten, twenty years later? Do you wish you had made some sacrifices five or ten years ago so that you would have an easier time today? Do you think you make better choices today than you did ten years ago?

11

Sometimes sacrifices have to be made. Are you willing to make them? The power of your financial future is in your hands.

* * *

Not yet eighteen, Dad enlisted in the Army. He was inducted and sent into the 101st Airborne division. Always a quick learner and keen on reading and educating himself, it was recognized that Dad had skills that were needed elsewhere. He was tested and sent to OCS (Officer's Candidate School) at Fort Benning, Georgia, where his penchant for understanding radio and Morse code led to him becoming a radio officer in the 8th Army, 4th Division.

After months in England preparing for the invasion of Europe, my father and a few hundred thousand of his buddies set out in the largest armada ever assembled for the assault on the beaches of Normandy. On June 6, 1944, Dad exited an LST sitting in the back of a jeep with his radio on his back. The 4th Division landed on Utah Beach. At this point, he was the radio officer for the commander of the 4th Division, Colonel James A. Van Fleet. (Later promoted to general, Van Fleet was described by President Harry S. Truman as "the greatest general we ever had.")

Months later after enough experiences to fill another book, Dad was airlifted to England. Although he was not wounded by gunfire, Dad was awarded the Purple Heart because his feet were frozen in the Battle of the Bulge. First to England for weeks of recovery, then back to America via New York, Dad was eventually mustered out at Ft. Hood in Texas.

(You may find it interesting that my dad's name, Famous, led him to becoming a champion boxer in the Fourth Army. My grandmother, who could not read or write and spoke little English, heard the word used to describe a well-known doctor. In French, the word has a beautiful, soft sound that she liked. Since she thought it was the doctor's name, that is what she named my father. During his youth, there was always a wise guy or bully who thought he could rile Dad by making fun of his name. So he had to become a boxer. By the way, Dad won most of his bouts by knockout because he was very strong and was double-jointed in his

wrists. *He also said nearly every opponent made fun of his name.)*

After nearly ten years of being away in the CCCs and then the Army, Dad returned to work on the farm. While he'd been gone, the beautiful, second-youngest daughter of my maternal grandparents had grown into a tall, dark-eyed beauty. Less than three months after his return from Europe, my mother and father were married. Nine months later, on September 22, 1946, their first son was born. A charter member of the baby boomer generation, I had now arrived. Over the next eight years, Glenn, Carl, and Greg filled out our growing family.

Like millions of baby boomers, my youth was one filled with family and friends. A college education was not considered absolutely necessary nor was it considered a right. Many GI's returning from overseas at the end of the war could not avail themselves of the GI Bill because conditions were desperate at home. They needed to go to work to help their parents and siblings who had experienced various levels of deprivation during the war years.

Learning the Lessons
of Youth

W hen I look back on the lives of my parents and grand-parents I am struck by the fact that they were, first of all, simple people. Please do not mistake this for ignorant; they were very well-read and accomplished in many ways.

The first thing I remember my dad telling me is *Never stop learning. Keep reading. Be a good reader and you will never stop learning all of your life.* Dad has, to this day, lived a life where he continues, even at age eighty-eight, to learn new things every day.

LESSON 4: Form useful habits.

It is said that it takes twenty-one days to form a new habit. That is true whether it involves a diet plan, quitting smoking, or an exercise routine. Once a new habit has become ingrained, it becomes virtually automatic. If for any reason you are not able to perform the established routine, you may feel compelled to reestablish it as soon as possible.

Baby boomers were taught that they should get an education, acquire a job, and make money. We were seldom taught that we must set aside time to manage that money. In fact, we did not believe that money could be managed, although we did learn how to spend it.

We spend many hours attempting to make money. Doesn't it make sense to spend thirty minutes to an hour each week managing your money? Is it worth the effort to insure that you make the wisest use of your personal assets? This is a useful habit that pays for itself.

At first you may find that you will spend more than an hour. With all the information and tools available through the Internet, you may spend hours doing research. But remember, this should not be done until you have first realistically evaluated your own current financial situation. You should also be sure that you have created a budget that honestly states your income and expenses (there are some great tools for this in the Appendix). Once you have done these things the time spent doing research will be directed and you will waste fewer hours chasing windmills on the Internet. Your research should be as focused as possible for each session.

For example, if the subject that you choose for the current research session is *online trading*, you should limit your time to that topic. During the following week you may find that you will take note of anything that relates to *online trading*. You will soon begin to see that the useful habit you are establishing is beginning to pay dividends.

Of course, the following week you will select a new topic to research, such as 401(k)s, mutual funds, stocks, investment opportunities, and so forth. You should continue to move along to different topics so that you become broadly informed on many matters that can positively and/or negatively affect your PRA. As time goes by, you may actually become an expert in one or more area of expertise.

As you expand your understanding of money matters, you will begin to realize that you can indeed be an expert when it comes to your own PRA. Then, when you select a financial planner or advisor to work with, you will be knowledgeable and capable of not only asking the right questions but, more importantly, directing the strategy that you wish to follow. Any competent advisor would appreciate working with you as an informed manager of your own money, your own PRA.

After a few weeks you will find that you have settled on a strategy that makes sense for you. If you have carefully read this book and adopted the suggestions, you will begin to understand how all of this relates to your own personal circumstance. You will set reasonable goals and benchmarks to measure your progress. As you review your PRA each week and see progress, however small, you will begin to become more proficient in managing money. It will become easier and soon you will realize that in thirty minutes or less each week you will stay in control of your PRA.

Is it worth it to form useful habits? The answer is obvious—the only question for anyone is whether you are willing and determined enough to do so. The best approach is to set reasonable, attainable goals and then not let anything prevent you from reaching them. It will soon become fun, rewarding, and profitable. The time you spend reading this book is part of forming those useful habits. There are lessons and sections that you will refer back to again and again. This book is not intended as a one-time read. It can be a continuing source of education, inspiration, and ideas. Your personal success in managing your PRA is my greatest satisfaction. Begin now to form useful financial habits. It is only twenty-one days from pain to gain!

* * *

My father returned to farming after the war but that old adage— "How can you keep them down on the farm after they've seen Paris?"—accurately describes his experience. My parents didn't stay on the farm for long. After working with the railroads for several years and building houses, at forty-two years of age Dad began working in a giant new valve plant built in our hometown. He started at the bottom rung on the burr bench just to get into the plant. He quickly rose through the ranks and several years later, Dad went into the inspections department. After learning the ropes, he became the chief inspector over the department approving all manner of valves, including those used in the nuclear industry. With his third grade education Dad now had a number of engineers and other college graduates working for him. They adored him and were constantly amazed at his ability to come up with complex mathematical answers using his own system and his great memory.

LESSON 5: It's never too late to start over.

Can it be said that it's all over for the baby boomer generation? Are we ready to throw in the towel and say, "We tried but the system beat us"? Is the baby boomer generation ready to ride quietly off into the sunset and simply absorb or suck the life out of what we think is left of the social security system, the environment, and institutions?

I don't think so. At our age, we are under no illusion with regard to the transitory benefit of material things, titles, and awards. We have learned that life is best lived when we do it with purpose and integrity. We have learned that giving of ourselves brings greater happiness than accumulating things.

What are we to do? How can we take at least some measure of control back so that we can live a more meaningful life? It's simpler than you think.

Follow my father's third grade advice: keep reading, keep learning—and become an expert regarding retirement.

Don't allow money to rule your life—get control and make money work for you. There are many excellent books on the subject, but realize that it may mean overthrowing some strongly entrenched beliefs and concepts.

Be ready to change—don't believe it when you are told you are at retirement age. What does that have to do with passion, with your purpose and mission in life?

Simplify your life by placing value on what is most important. Do not be concerned about image, avoid pretense, and do not imagine that you have all the answers.

Remember the days of your youth when solving problems and facing challenges was part of the excitement and thrill of life? Get busy and start solving them while always remembering that the decisions we made as baby boomers are now bearing fruit. The Bible says in Galatians 6:7 to be careful about what we sow because good or bad, we are surely going to reap based on what we sow. That is certainly true for our generation.

One of the greatest things that the baby boomer generation can realize and embrace is that there is still work to do! So what if you don't have a retirement. Are you going to just allow your bad decisions to make you cynical and desperate? Is this generation going to just dump on its children and grandchildren? And if there is still work to do, what is it? What can we do to add purpose and meaning to our lives and not become a burden on our children and society in general?

The answers to those questions are waiting to be answered—and the answers may be different for each one of us. But finding answers and solutions means that we are involved, energetic, and inspired. We are not ready to be thrown out the back door of some poorly managed corporation or corrupt institution and be left behind like yesterday's newspaper. There is more to be heard from the baby boomer generation. Over the next several years the experience, knowledge, and desire of this generation will create waves of change. Whether that change is beneficial or not will largely depend upon your point of view and how you are able to cope with different circumstances.

One of the most amazing trends seen today is the emergence of Asia as a booming generator of capital and investment. Although some Western countries are experiencing low or zero growth rates, at this writing, China continues to surge at an approximately 10 percent growth rate.

The advent of the Internet has made it possible for the enormous human capital available on the Asian continent to impact world economies in ways no one could have imagined just a few years ago. The economic potential of Asia is incredible and will likely afford many opportunities over the next few years.

In a speech to more than 1,800 delegates at the seventh annual Boao Forum for Asia (BOAO) on April 20, 2007, Bill Gates stated that Asia has the potential to lead the way for global economic improvement. He based this on the growing availability of the Internet and Asia's determination to grow while avoiding many of the pitfalls of the past. He also said cooperative efforts, through Microsoft and the Bill and Melinda Gates Foundation, were being made to insure that in the future each and every Asian student will have access to his own affordable computer. He also said he expects that the next great technological innovation will come from Asia.

The attendees of the BFA conference were a cross-section of baby boomers from around the globe. This generation will continue to remain engaged and on the cutting edge of innovation and implementation. It is not insignificant to note, also, that Asian culture has a strong component of honor and respect for seniors.

But remember the entire point of this narrative is one baby boomer's quest for a satisfying and fulfilling retirement situation in a world with ever more rapidly changing pressures. The work to do in this regard will surely revolve around three things that it is imperative you recognize:

The need to access and utilize information. This is especially true regarding the stock markets, and the tools and guiding principles to successfully manage your own portfolio with assistance from Certified Financial Planners and Registered Investment Advisors. (Remembering, of course, that no one has all the answers.)

The understanding that past business models often no longer work like we were taught they should. What's happened in the recording industry is a classic example of an industry that held on to a dying business model.

In the past, record labels discovered a musician, recorded an album, promoted and marketed it, and sold albums in traditional retail outlets (stores). The company paid for everything, and the company made most of the profits too. But with the advent of technology and the downsizing of both the size and price of that technology (remember what a hand-held calculator *used* to cost?), some musicians bought their own recording equipment and made their own recordings. This allowed them to control the musical results, gave them the freedom to record songs that the record label might not have deemed worthy, and, most importantly, kept them out of hock with the record company. They owned their own masters and controlled their own product.

But what about all that promoting and marketing? That business model was changing too. The Internet was adopted by artists of all ages to promote their music through personal Web sites and social networking sites such as MySpace. They could sell their music direct to consumers. And in the meantime, traditional retail outlets were suffering as online retailers such as Amazon cut prices and offered a wide selection. When Apple's iTunes Store started offering single songs for sale as a digital download, some thought album sales would disappear completely.

They haven't—but that's because the record companies quit fighting the revolution and started using it instead.

The fact of the matter is that the business world is in constant flux; everything changes. Therefore, we cannot depend upon companies, industries, or institutions (government or private) to guarantee our retirement.

We must learn to work together with like-minded people to secure answers and solutions. Collaboration—not conflict … teamwork—not climbing the corporate ladder … admitting mistakes—not concealing defeats … all of these things are the keys to getting the work done.

So what are you going to do? Are you just going to wait for the dire predictions regarding retirement to descend upon you? Do you recognize that there are still opportunities and options? Only you can answer those questions. As for me, I intend to embrace my age, be thankful for the health I still have, put important things first in my life and go forward with purpose. After all, there is still work to do!

* * *

At sixty-two, Dad retired and for sixteen years spent his life caring for Mom, doing volunteer work, and becoming a learned student of the Bible. When he went to visit the plant, at least once a year, all the old-timers would quickly find him, picking up old conversations right where they left off. My father's retirement life was full and had purpose because he never stopped learning and being fascinated with life. Although he had a comfortable retirement, he was never considered rich during his lifetime, nor did he live in luxury. But he had wealth beyond measure and contentment with his circumstances.

LESSON 6: A simple life really works.

Living a simple life includes not overburdening yourself with debt while you try to keep up with some elusive image of what others think of you. It means being content with what you have. Living a simple life does not mean you can't have a life of abundance. Indeed, there are now books and magazines devoted to the notion of living simply yet with style. Living within your means, however, affects so much more than just your financial well-being.

Gabe Renzo, age sixty-three, of Dearborn Heights, Michigan, was quoted in a *USA Today* article entitled, "Securing Your Retirement" on September 24, 2007. He said, "Young people today don't save money, and the main reason they don't is that they're overburdened by debt. This is the only generation that will drive to the poorhouse in a BMW."

The corollary to this lesson is to let go of any attempts at pretension. It is not necessary to attempt to be something you are not. This doesn't imply that you should not try to improve. It simply means not to put on airs but to take a realistic appraisal of yourself and find satisfaction in who you are and where you came from.

* * *

Desperation and concern for the future have been magnified in the lives of the baby boomer generation; those almost idyllic days of the mid-1950s had started to fade the day the Russians put Sputnik into orbit in 1957.

Early one morning in mid-October 1962, we awoke to a sound I had never heard before. It was wave after wave of B-52 bombers and fighter aircraft taking off from England Air Force Base in my hometown of Alexandria, Louisiana, headed for Florida and regions surrounding Cuba. The Cuban missile crisis was now fully engaged. We had heard of the call-up of the National Guard on the evening news the night before. The crescendo of those aircraft overhead on that clear morning signaled a change in circumstances that has molded the lives of baby boomers since that day.

The remainder of the 1960s was like a blur. My graduation from high school in 1964 was a signal event in our family. That was put into perspective by the assassination of President Kennedy the year before, the growing conflict in Southeast Asia, followed by one political assassination after another through the end of the 1960s.

There were so many upheavals that occurred during this period that it has become, perhaps, the most scrutinized decade of the twentieth century. Many forces came to the fore during those times that have served to apply added pressure on the baby boomer generation. The idea of free love gave root to the hippie movement, which was really a manifestation of the rejection of the status quo in society. The boomer generation lost many members during this time due to the war in Viet Nam. Several of my childhood friends lost their lives in Viet Nam. The heated public discourse of the day left many with little hope for the future.

The grief, heartache, and suffering that resulted in rejection of authority culminated with the advent of the God-is-dead proponents. Religion began to lose its hold as many baby boomers threw themselves into satisfying their urges and desires to the fullest. With the seemingly unstoppable encroachment of communism, religion's influence and ability to impact the everyday lives of baby boomers and their children decreased.

Time and unforeseen occurrence were kind to me. The solid upbringing and spiritual strength of my family enabled me to keep focused on the important things in life. It seemed that many people were now seeking just their own interests. Selfish personal aggrandizement came to the fore and narcissistic thinking eventually led to baby boomers being described as the Me Generation.

The lives of all baby boomers have been influenced by conflicting agendas, challenges to long held truths and an overriding re-

alization that things were never going to be like the mid-1950s again. The need to be careful and not find ourselves consumed by a world gone totally materialistic could only be realized if we had a good sense of what is important in life. When I refer back to the lessons of youth, I have never failed to be content when I realize that I only need to be what I am, not being pretentious or exalted in my opinion of myself.

However, that has been a huge challenge for me and for this generation. We can relate to what Benjamin Franklin is purported to have said: "Alas, each time I feel I have achieved humility, I am proud of it."

Beyond A Formal Education

*D*ad always said a recession is when someone else is out of work or doesn't have a job adequate to support his family; a depression is when you are out of work and can't support your family. During my last three years of high school, I was able to gain some valuable experience in business. I worked part-time while going to school and helped Dad pay some expenses during a period of depression for our family.

At graduation there were offers of scholarships and further formal education but two paths opened for me. The first offered the opportunity to engage in a volunteer work that I was passionate about and would lead to the full-time ministry; the second would lead to a career in business that would allow me to continue to help my family financially. I chose to do both, spending dedicated time in my volunteer work and working part-time.

This has resulted in a life-long process of balancing the need to make money and keeping those things I view as most important paramount in my life. I do not regret any part of that effort, as it has kept me grounded during the worst of times. But if I'd had training in managing finances and some knowledge of investments, that would have made the process much easier. It would have also allowed me to prepare better for my retirement years. Although I would not exchange the exciting and rewarding experiences I have *enjoyed or the friendships I have made for a larger savings account, you could still avoid some of my mistakes by learning more about how to invest—and how not to.*

LESSON 7: The stock market is a two-edged sword.

It is said, regarding stockbrokers and traders, that they cannot predict the future. They must always couch their suggestions with the disclaimer that *losses can and do occur.* The shelter of protection provided investors by virtue of government oversight organizations should give investors confidence. The necessary compliance issues that stockbrokers and traders must factor in daily should translate into an additional layer of protection for investors.

Who can deny that the stock market has produced incredible returns for millions of investors? Who can deny that over the long haul the stock market generally provides gain? Who can deny that the stockbrokers and traders, the ones who most understand the markets, are the ones who garner the greatest gain from the movement of the markets? Why were all the major houses touting, recommending, and buying Enron stock the week prior to Enron's demise? Why hasn't the American public not fully accepted their stockbrokers' insistence that they cannot predict the future? Is there any better methodology or instrument of measurement that is available to the average investor who would like to share in the success of the American marketplace? Why do so many continue to invest in the markets when they are subjecting their retirement to stockbrokers and traders who admit that they could not predict Enron or the dot-com disaster or any other major shifts in the marketplace?

And why, then, do so many investors wander through the maze of intricacies without the slightest understanding of what really makes the markets work? With every other major financial decision in life, investors typically retain the decision making power for themselves. They pride themselves in being savvy, having done their homework, and they make decisions based upon the best information available. Is it really all just a big gamble and should investors really look at their investments into the market as money they are willing to lose?

For millions of baby boomers and me, it is time to start building on reality. We do not have the time, now, to make the Rule of 72 work for us that we did twenty or thirty years ago. We have tried everything the experts suggested to us. Many of us have succeeded beyond our wildest dreams. And yet the majority of us—the first of the baby boom generation—have arrived at this time without a retirement income or strategy for retirement. Please understand that by retirement I mean the freedom to choose what to do with your life and time. That may well include continuing to do work that is fulfilling, rewarding, and satisfying. It may be a complete departure from your previous career path. It may be fulfilling a lifelong dream or doing something noble or worthwhile, such as spending more of your time in pursuits that are voluntary and self-sacrificing.

But there are facts that our generation must face. We have to believe that there is at least some truth to the statements that the Social Security net has gaping holes in it and cannot be relied on to provide for our retirement. Simply stated, we have beaten the statistical analysis for our generation. We are too healthy and we are living too long. At a time when we wish to follow the path of our parents' generation—that is, retirement to pursue our life's passions—we can only look forward to continuing to compete in the workplace for our piece of the action. Many baby boomers no longer view retirement as an option. Many of my friends say we will have more time to visit when we work together as greeters at Wal-Mart.

We baby boomers can be rightly charged with missing some of the lessons of youth. We have not lived a more 'simple' life like some of our parents. We felt we deserved all that the information age said we were entitled to. Since, as teenagers, we lived through the 1960s with the threat of nuclear war hanging over us, we felt we had to have things now and our generation went after instant gratification. We willingly exchanged our future retirement for the pursuit of our desires.

With all of these perplexing thoughts floating in our heads, is it any wonder that many of the baby boomer generation feel overwhelmed by all the information swamping our subconscious minds? Where do we turn for reliable information related to our potential investments and the ability to create at least a measure of retirement?

My quest for the answers to all these questions has taken me from coast to coast and has included discussions with some of the most renowned authorities of our times. For the past five years I have attended seminars and met with some of the most notable financial advisors and planners in the United States. While there is much agreement about basic precepts, there is disagreement respecting specific strategies. And—of even greater concern to consumers—*the fees and/or commissions relative to a particular recommendation drive many advisors and planners.*

One group in particular, through the use of excellent marketing, regularly convenes seventy or more potential investors, generally at country clubs around the nation. They provide the guests with snacks or a light meal, present a slide presentation anywhere from forty-five minutes to an hour and a half in length, and then proceed to close deals right on the spot. Because of this group's efforts to recruit me as a presenter, I got to learn an interesting fact. At the conclusion of each program after all guests have departed, they calculate their "take," which generally ranged in the neighborhood of $200,000 and higher. I am not talking about investment dollars—I am talking about commissions earned when the deals started that evening were consummated. While being compensated for providing consumers valuable information and advice is an acceptable practice, the field is rife with opportunists whose real purpose is to separate baby boomers from their hard-earned savings and, in some cases, a significant percentage of their future earnings.

So the importance of educating yourself about investment opportunities cannot be overstated. Generally accepted themes that are prevalent today include:

- The need to diversify.
- The need to be educated about the Rule of 72.
- The stock markets generally trend upward.
- The need to get moving with investments—time is critical.

On the other hand, themes not so readily understood are:

- The need for individuals to exercise control of their investments.
- The fact that mutual funds are not the secure instruments generally believed.
- The fact that 401(k)s include substantial risks.

There are new criteria for evaluating stocks that are available to individual investors; these criteria have proven track records in identifying stocks with superior earnings. Again, it is not too late for baby boomers to secure an improved retirement position.

Building on reality has never been more difficult than it is for the boomer generation. We are simply overwhelmed with choices, options, conflicting opinions, and agendas. Experts eloquently argue for their diametrically opposed conclusions and recommendations.

There are several things you can do that will help narrow down and pick out those strategies that you feel are best for your situation. First, you must educate yourself sufficiently with basic financial truths and principles. This will expose most of the inaccurate, false, and misleading self-styled experts. Additionally, it will greatly advance your cause if you have identified at least one trusted financial advisor or coach with whom you can communicate your questions and concerns.

Once you've identified a strategy, perform a "pilot program." For example, with stocks, create a "watch account" that you can monitor. Then, place only a portion of your available investment assets into the vehicle of choice and monitor its activity carefully for a sufficient period to benchmark results. Your stockbroker or Registered Investment Advisor (RIA) can assist you in understanding how this may work best for you.

Although you may have great trust in your advisor, continue to be interested in and involved in the management of your stock portfolio. No one will have greater interest or motivation than you do with respect to your own portfolio.

Just as you would study *Consumer Reports* prior to purchasing a product, spend some time keeping up with investment trends and information. You spend years or a lifetime building up assets; you must spend some time to protect and grow those assets. If not, you will surely waste them or lose them.

Educate yourself regarding the truth about mutual funds and 401(k)s and the relative risks to your retirement. There may well be options that are safer, more stable, more diversified and that provide greater returns. The fact is that there is much evidence to suggest the need to be skeptical about the claims of mutual funds and 401(k)s. This information is part of the public domain but is buried beneath all the hype supplied by the various funds. The potential dangers are usually so obscure within the information that it takes, as they say, a Philadelphia lawyer to figure it out. Of course, there are some examples of superior returns but, as they must legally tell you, "Past performance is no guarantee of future returns."

A study by the Employee Benefit Research Institute, based in Washington DC, determined that some 32 percent of workers above the age of fifty-five have retirement savings of less than $25,000. This fact only emphasizes the need for us to deal in reality. How many may only have less than $50,000? How much do you think you will need for your retirement?

Building on reality takes time and effort. The rewards are plentiful. The greatest risk that you will run is having long cherished ideas or dogmas proven false. The reward may well be a more enjoyable, fulfilling, and purposeful retirement.

* * *

Dad's advice to never quit learning was my guiding compass. I read voraciously and went from one subject of interest to another. It has been said that a man might read one book on a subject and be informed, he might read ten books on the subject and be an expert, and then read fifty books on the subject and be considered an authority. I have always been curious and wanted to know what is behind doors—what goes on in various factories and industry, corporations, hospitals, and government agencies has always interested me. Through the years I have been fortunate and have availed myself of opportunities to quench much of that curiosity while always absorbing, learning, and expanding.

After getting married in 1966, I started a small business to pro-vide for the needs of my new family. Within a year and a half I had built a business that was so successful that I was able to sell it for what was a princely sum at the time. That success was built around a janitorial business. What I learned about running a business dur-ing that time provided the basis for my next venture.

By 1975 I had built a new business that was both the number one and fastest growing franchised operation in its industry. With a desire to spend more time in my volunteer work, I once again had the opportunity to sell a business and did so in 1981.

Abiding by the noncompete feature of my agreement, I left Lou-isiana with my wife and three-year-old son, heading for the moun-tains of North Carolina. Over the next several years, during the 1980s, I built two businesses. Like many of us baby boomers, I had success upon success to the extent that many of my friends and asso-ciates began to say that everything I touched turned to gold.

Because of my success with the franchise I sold in Louisiana, I was given the opportunity of opening a new franchised operation in western North Carolina. We launched the business in 1982 and by 1985 I once again had the fastest growing franchise in the country. Just three years after opening, the franchisor was building a new model and needed to reacquire franchise territories. The president of the company offered to buy back my franchise, although the original rights had been granted me at no cost. It didn't take long for me to accept that offer.

Shortly after that, I had the opportunity to acquire some prop-erties that led to a very successful business that included develop-ing properties, becoming one of the fastest growing contractors in the region, owning a real estate company, and closing mortgage loans with major banks.

LESSON 8: Buy land.

In the lifetime of the baby boomer generation, there is an activity that has generated some of the most compelling success stories and also some of the most catastrophic failures—that of investing in land and property. As some wizened old ones have counseled, "They ain't making no more land."

During the 1980s, buying, selling, and developing properties was at the core of much of the financial success that I enjoyed. Any failure was a direct result of poor decisions. It was certainly not because investing in this earth was a wrong strategy. Of course, it bears reminding ourselves that our possession of any portion of land is temporary and limited. However, investing in land and/or property does provide some of the best potential return, which can allow us to create an estate and meaningful retirement.

Today there are a myriad of courses and seminars that can provide us with information and ideas that we may never have had time to learn for ourselves. So we can accelerate our understanding of time-proven strategies. On my desk right now is an invitation to a seminar called the Creating Wealth Summit. This seminar is produced by the real estate billionaire Donald J. Trump, and is entitled "Creating Wealth the Trump Way."

While a seminar like this can be helpful, you still have to carefully weigh any new or different investment strategies in relation to your overall financial picture and goals. With regard to land or property, the average investor often learns about excellent investment opportunities too late. However, in a growing economy and an area of rising values, you can often find investments that will work for you.

All of this takes effort, and you must invest sufficient time so that you can make a decision quickly when the opportunity presents itself. There are many examples of individual investors who have had rags to riches stories because they educated themselves and wisely invested in land or property. One of the best of these that I know of is an individual I consider one of my mentors.

In the late 1970s a hard-working gentleman owned and managed a service station in the Biltmore area of Asheville, North Carolina. He provided the best, most hospitable service to all of his clients, which included some of the wealthiest people in the area. To this day, many Asheville natives remember that service station with fondness. It reminds them of a bygone era that, sadly, our grandchildren will never know. This was a time when people still gathered around at service stations, grocery stores, or other such locations to exchange ideas, views, and just tell stories.

This fine man never forgot his humble beginnings. But, as the years passed and with the help and advice of many of his friends and mentors, he gradually acquired properties and land. As time went by, he found it necessary to go into the real estate business full-time and launched his own real estate company. As he did so, he continued to acquire property.

In the mid-1980s, he began to develop some of the properties he had acquired. He always drew to his side young, energetic, entrepreneurial people and allowed them to succeed along with him. His signature properties led the way to a renaissance of development, particularly in the south part of Asheville.

In the late 1980s his son returned from college to join the business with his father. He had been a star baseball pitcher in college and was extremely motivated to excel and gain his father's smile of approval. Today, the business that started in a service station has grown to become one of the most significant development organizations in western North Carolina. With the father's continuing vision and the day-to-day management provided by his son, their business continues to thrive and enrich Asheville.

You should note that the success described above came with much effort and learning the ropes, spread out over four decades. Many of us in the baby boomer generation continue to look for the quick hit, the easy fix, or the lottery. Some like to say that success like that my friend enjoyed is just luck. They completely overlook all that went into his success.

So when you think about investing in land or property, remember that in most cases, it will take some time for you to realize dramatic returns. If you are alert and remain informed, you may, from time to time, come upon a deal that makes you a lot of money quickly. You might even be able to turn a property in a short period of time. I had a property that I sold the same day that I bought it and doubled my money. To make this work I had to be informed, ready to pull the trigger, and I had to have the money to make it happen instantly.

Something interesting you should know is that when most people talk about this sort of thing, it is the exception rather than the rule. Unless you really know what you are doing, the potential for disaster lies with moving too quickly. Often the best deal is to make no deal at all. Watch out for overinflated values, promises with nothing in writing, and a push to get you to buy without proper inspection or evaluation. It may be too good to be true because the property really is not as valuable as you are being influenced to believe.

On the other hand, I had the opportunity to buy fifty acres adjoining the city limits of a major city. The land was not listed or on the market. I learned about the land as I got to know some of the local residents in the area by visiting them at their homes. I found that the heirs of this property lived out of state and really had little interest in the property, as it appeared to have limited access.

However, on investigation and after having walked the entire property with an engineer and my grading contractor, I contacted the attorney for the owners and made an offer to buy. I didn't try to offer them the absolute lowest price that I believe it could have been bought for. In other words I did not try to "steal" the property. Instead, I offered them a fair price that still represented a very good deal for me.

My offer was accepted the very next day. I was able to develop a small subdivision of forty-five lots that is now within the city limits and has become one of the most desirable developments in the area. Because of being prepared, having done the work of properly evaluating the property, and having the money to move quickly, I was able to experience superior returns. And, I got a lot of personal pleasure out of keeping the property as natural as possible, with the least damage to trees and the environment.

There are several other areas of investment opportunity with regard to land and property that you should include in your research. One such subject has to do with tax-deferred exchanges or "1031 exchanges." Your financial planner, real estate, and/or tax attorney can all be a help to you in analyzing potential benefits.

If you have property with value in your portfolio but it is located in another state or area you may wish to take a look at a possible 1031 exchange. There may be some property nearby that better suits your interests if you wish to have more direct involvement with its management or development. There are other reasons why you may elect to do a 1031 Exchange. Depending on your circumstances, this may be very helpful to you as you grow and manage your PRA.

The theory behind Section 1031 is that when a property owner has reinvested the sale proceeds into another property, the economic gain has not been realized in a way that generates funds to pay any tax. In other words, the taxpayer's investment is still the same, only the form has changed (e.g. vacant land exchanged for apartment building). Therefore, it would be unfair to force the taxpayer to pay tax on a "paper" gain. In a typical property sale, an owner usually has to pay taxes on any gain. In a properly executed transaction, the realized tax is deferred. These transactions are sanctioned under Section 1031 of the Internal Revenue Code and are often referred to as 1031 exchanges, like-kind exchanges, or tax-deferred exchanges.

A 1031 exchange allows property owners to postpone taxes on the sale of investment property, provided that property is exchanged for like-kind investment property of an equal or greater value. The property may be vacant land, rental property, or property used for trade, business, or investment. See Appendix C for other pertinent points about a 1031 exchange.

Should you work with a realtor? Competent realtors can be worth everything you pay them. They can be your best friend. I have found that working with realtors can multiply your efforts. But they are no substitute for doing your own homework. Quite often I have found that my vision for the beneficial use of a property was spot-on, while realtors did not see what I did.

With regard to one property, I was told, "Don't buy or build in that area. Nothing good happens there and look at the distressed properties in that neighborhood." In this case the entire realtor community overlooked the fact that a prime four-lane connector highway with access was within two blocks of my targeted property. The property fronted onto the main four-lane highway with obvious great visibility. I also had done my homework and knew that rental properties were in great demand in that area because it had excellent access from the other side to the University of North Carolina–Asheville (UNCA).

Nonetheless, I bought it. This was over the objection of various realtors and bankers. My company designed and built a twenty-unit apartment complex. During the construction phase I enlisted my preferred real estate company to rent the apartments, but they *still* did not see my vision and they failed. So I decided to just rent the units myself and at the rental price that the realtors thought was too high.

In the course of the six months of construction on the project, I rented all the units and had a waiting list of potential renters. All the units were rented at my projected rental price. By the time the project was completed I had several investors, some from out of state, who were interested in purchasing the project. On Christmas Eve of that year I closed on the sale of this project that all the local realtors said could not be done. They said it could not be rented and to top it off they said I would not sell it for my asking price— yet my buyer was thrilled to close on his new apartment complex at my asking price. I consummated other more profitable land ventures, but this one brought me a lot of personal satisfaction. The purchase and subsequent development of that part of the property allowed me to make available another section of property to be used to construct a new place of worship. In addition, I earned over a quarter of a million dollars on this project.

Purchasing a property in a distressed condition does expose you to more risk. Most of the time investors and realtors will shy away from the prospect of being the first to develop in such an area. But if you have done your homework and if you have a vision based on good information, your return may be significant.

In no way is the foregoing meant to discredit realtors. All of this should go to confirm to you that whatever you are investing in, you had better be personally involved. No one will have the incentive that you do to make a plan work.

There are two kinds of realtors with whom I have been able to create synergy. One is the new, young, energetic agent who is working hard to partner with clients and investors. The other is the longtime, very established, professional realtor who knows everyone in a given market area. The former gives you energy and a can-do spirit and often uncovers heretofore unseen opportunities.

The latter gives you a solid basis for understanding property values in his or her area of expertise.

If it is your intention to invest in land or property on a continuing basis, do seek to create synergy or a strategic partnership with a competent realtor. At times you may do a deal without her, but if you are continuing to give your realtor some business and keeping her informed of what you are doing, she will often be glad to offer suggestions or helpful comments. In other words, treat her the way you would like to be treated. Perhaps you thought I might neglect to mention that very important lesson, but no. That is the real way things should work and actually do work best.

The strategy you select for investing in land and property in general should be the one that allows you the greatest opportunity to experience the highest rate of return in the shortest period of time. Remember the Rule of 72, which you can refer to in Appendix B. Sometimes it is better to divest oneself of land or property and utilize another instrument that best suits your needs. Work closely with your chosen investment advisor as you make these important choices.

* * *

In 1987, I was presented with a prestigious business award before an audience of more than one thousand business owners. It was the pinnacle of success in business and proved that there is life beyond a formal education. You will have no trouble believing that it was hard not to be swayed by the accolades. Some of it may have been deserved, but no one succeeds solely because of his own efforts. Oh, he may be the catalyst and may provide the initial energy, but it takes the efforts and support of many to breed lasting success.

It was about this time that my father was asked about his successful son. His comment was loaded with meaning, while also demonstrating the satirical humor that he possessed until the day he died. Dad demonstrated what he meant by moving his hand up and down as he said, "Yes, my son has been successful and I am proud of him. You know he is the first one in our family to escape the poverty level and he has escaped it three times."

How true that proved to be when just two years later, in 1989, I took on a project that eventually led to the demise of my very successful company and the loss of millions of dollars! There is nothing in my narrative to this point that would indicate to you that my father was a financial wizard or that he had built any kind of fortune. However, in 1987, at the height of my success, I told Dad exactly where I was financially. His advice to me was prophetic. He said, "Son, get out now. Don't take on any more contracts. You should never have to work again. You can pursue your passion in life. Make your life simple again."

It is true that only later in life do we realize just how much our parents actually did know and how much we should have listened to them. I remember all too well my response: "Dad, I will just take on this one more project. It will last for over a year and will allow me to wind things down. Thank you for the advice and I will work toward doing what you suggested."

It saddens me to admit the real reason I did not follow my father's advice. At that point, I had far exceeded any accomplishments of my dad—or so it seemed. I never felt he was anything but a good man, but he had never run a business or achieved the acclaim and success that I had. While well-meaning, he just didn't understand what an opportunity I had before me. I really thought this would be my last project and then I would retire to pursue what I consider more important things.

When I went home to visit, I saw some of my old school chums. Some of them had gone on to a formal education, had graduated from college and were working as firemen, teachers, in retail stores, or fast food operations. There is certainly nothing wrong with any of those careers. But, with just a couple of exceptions, I did not know of anyone from my graduating class that had accomplished anything close to what I had achieved financially.

I had even built the house of our dreams overlooking Asheville, North Carolina. The home had won the Grand Award for Design as chosen by the Association of General Contractors (AGC). It was highlighted in the first-ever four-color edition of the local Asheville Citizen Times, with numerous color photographs and an article praising the project. Other projects received similar treatment after this, with several additional awards being won by my company.

After reflecting on some of these things, I decided in my heart that Dad's advice, while well meant, was just wrong at this time in my life. It seems that we all make decisions in life that don't lead to the conclusion that we anticipated. You need some background information to understand some of the things that influenced my decision relative to that last project.

In 1987 we had completed our beautiful home high up at 4,000 feet overlooking the city of Asheville, North Carolina. It was hailed as the highest home on the Asheville water system. The panoramic view encompassed 270 degrees for a distance of approximately sixty miles to the Great Smokey Mountains. With its 108-foot long deck overlooking the valley below, we could watch the seasons pass. We could see the snow moving across Mount Pisgah as it descended into the valley containing Asheville, past the Biltmore House and up the mountain until we were engulfed.

On clear nights during the winter, we could, on occasion, get a glimpse of the Aurora Borealis. We saw meteor showers from that wonderful vantage point. The previous year we had come up to the property and observed the passing of Halley's comet on a crystal clear night. On summer nights we could sit on the deck enjoying the gentle breezes coming up the mountain; we would sit there with our growing son, excitedly discussing the future and all it would bring.

Being the first ones to build in this development, we had the opportunity to watch new homes being built and get to know each of our neighbors. Most of them had read about our home and the awards we had won. Our nearest neighbor proved to be a very nice family. The wife was a stockbroker with one of the major firms in the country. Her family and her husband's family are very well known in the world of professional baseball and in the business community. She appeared to have great credibility.

I used to speak to her on occasion about investing in the stock market. Of course, nothing could compare to my businesses, where I routinely realized 40 percent returns on my investments (sometimes more). But in the back of my mind, the thought of diversifying was floating around. I had met some giants of industry and business and they'd said that diversification was vitally important. The problem was I didn't really know a competent financial planner. I am not sure that in the late 1980s I had even met one, although bankers and others were always giving me advice. My idea of diversification was starting another related business or buying more property.

Bear in mind where I had come from. From those humble beginnings in Louisiana to my large business and beautiful home sitting high up overlooking Asheville was a very long way. And it had been the product of hard work, common sense, and good timing. I felt I was justifiably proud of those accomplishments. What could investing in the stock market do for me? At that time the Dow had not hit 3,000. The future boom was not evident or even on the horizon.

One day my neighbor and I happened to be outside and admiring the view across the valley. It was a very pleasant summer day with gentle breezes as there always were, which, at that altitude, was very comfortable, even in the summer. We did not even require air conditioning in our house.

We sat down in the grass and I decided this was a good time to learn more about the stock market and the work my neighbor did. Our discussion was wide-ranging and very informative. It was clear that although my neighbor had come from a life of privilege, she had earned her stripes in the industry and was a competent stockbroker. I knew some of her clients and they all spoke highly of her.

We talked about how the market evaluated companies and why there were ups and downs in the market. Much of this was not foreign to me, but I was speaking to an expert so I listened with great interest. I inquired as to her view of the Great Depression and could we ever expect that again. I felt I was beginning an exploration of another new dimension that I knew virtually nothing about.

Just the previous year I had gone to insurance school and obtained my insurance license. It was not my goal to become an insurance agent, but since I bought so much insurance in the course of conducting business, I thought it was a good idea to better understand how insurance works and learn of advantages that might be available to my companies. My neighbor suggested that perhaps

I needed to seek to get a securities license. Thinking back on my insurance classes and because I had a growing interest, that seemed like a sensible suggestion.

Before I signed the contract for that last project, I began to think that maybe Dad and my wife were right. Maybe I should quit now and invest my money in the stock market. Perhaps, I should retire and work the assets and properties we already had in our portfolio. If I did that, I could give attention to the things that had my greatest interest in life.

As it turns out, everything that was to happen to me from that time, financially speaking, hinged on the next things that were said. I asked her, "Do you think the stock market will ever hit 3,000?" Her answer to this day resonates like a bell. This was a lady with credentials, conservative in her estimation of things, a great list of clients. Why was her answer not, at the very least, in the ballpark of what was to come? Would anyone think that this stockbroker would ever give an opinion that would be so far out of sync with the future reality of the stock market?

I did not realize that her answer would sway my decision in a way that would have unbelievable implications for the rest of my life. It would affect all future business decisions I would make, it would challenge our family for years, and set me on a course that has taken over fifteen years of searching to reach conclusions and understandings that I believe involve every baby boomer.

Her confident answer was, "Not in your lifetime!"

LESSON 9: Take steps to preserve the wealth you have.

What is the use of acquiring wealth and assets if they cannot be protected or used for some purpose of your choosing? Except for the financial upper crust of society, too few of us have been exposed to wealth preservation or protection strategies. There are so many legal options available. With the help of your financial planner you can learn more about what may work best for your situation.

The story you are reading about my life should prove to you the value of preserving or protecting wealth. That is part of the reason I am going to such lengths to describe the painful experiences that I've gone through only because I lacked knowledge in this area.

Horror stories abound about individuals who failed to protect their wealth. Please understand that what qualifies as wealth varies from one person to another. But you would be amazed at how many people with a net worth of a million or multimillions have done nothing to preserve their wealth. Would it not make sense to preserve what you have worked so hard for, regardless of its size?

One true story revolves around a famous country music star in Nashville, Tennessee. Conway Twitty's success had led to him accumulating some substantial wealth. He had even built a successful amusement park called Twitty City. Shortly before he died, Mr. Twitty changed his will and took his first wife out of it. He put his second wife and children into the will.

His first wife contested the will and won. This case is part of the public record on file at the courthouse in Hendersonville, Tennessee. Because he had not allowed for proper asset protection, it became necessary for his estate to be liquidated at less than thirty cents on the dollar. This resulted in a loss of between $10 to $12 million for the estate.

All of this could have been avoided if he had just made provision for wealth protection. Any one of a number of trusts could have protected his assets and preserved them for his intended heirs. A trust is an agreement under which money or other assets are held and managed by one person for the benefit of another. Different types of trusts may be created to accomplish specific goals. Each kind may vary in the degree of flexibility and control it offers.

I've listed a variety of trust options in Appendix D. There are many more and some are specific to certain states. It is essential that you identify a qualified financial planner that you have confidence in to help you in this area.

This list by no means covers all the available trust options. There is another entire area that involves offshore trusts and apparently they are the right vehicle for some. But in recent years, some of the benefits of offshore trusts seem to have diminished. So if that has your attention, be sure to be well informed prior to making any commitments.

Regardless, you should check with your financial planner or advisor for these and other means available for wealth preservation. It is impossible for you to have a secure retirement if you do not protect what you have already accumulated—no matter the amount. I cannot stress enough how important it is for you to do more research into the importance of wealth preservation. It can provide you with tangible benefits now while preparing for the future of your beneficiaries. In the case of unanticipated catastrophe or death, exercising some of these options may provide you and your family with peace of mind and some financial security.

The Boomer Is Busted

*I*n 1987, I was forty-one years of age with great health, and I had achieved some significant financial wealth and momentum. I had a track record of success and building wealth that had proved to me that it could be done the old-fashioned way—through hard work and applying sound business practices to each endeavor.

At that moment I decided to go forward with what I thought would be my last project. And the end result of that so-called last project was that instead of protecting and growing my assets during the time when the market began its meteoric climb in the 1990s, I had to divest myself of the very financial assets that could have allowed me to ride that wave. By the time the Dow had reached 3,000, contrary to my stockbroker friend's prognostications, I was back to square one. I had utilized all my cash, divested myself of my properties and, as a final stroke, sold my beautiful dream house for a fraction of what it was worth to a very happy couple retiring from San Francisco. We sold everything so that I could pay off the debt on that last project. At this point, I should have fired myself as an incompetent manager of my own portfolio!

LESSON 10: Make use of new ways to utilize the stock market.

Many baby boomers are convinced that investing in the stock market provides some of the greatest opportunity for generating higher returns. Of course, the flip side is the risk that is also present in the manner that stocks have been bought and sold in the past.

Stock pickers and analysts fill the airwaves and Internet with their latest and best winning picks. Talking heads loudly boast and preen as they establish themselves as the experts in the minds of consumers. The sad fact is that many of these so-called experts are not in the know at all. By the time they give recommendations the market has essentially moved on, based on facts that came to light after their selections were made.

Stockbrokers are primarily reactive rather than proactive. That is not entirely their fault. The system is set up that way. This doesn't suggest that stockbrokers do not make good recommendations. It just confirms to us that *we need to be involved and informed.*

To first understand the scope of the opportunity versus the risk, you must understand some of the recent developments related to the stock market. These stories should make clear the importance of being knowledgeable about your investments. You cannot afford to rely totally on popular advice.

For example, on November 28, 2001, the stock of Enron (a Houston, Texas, company whose demise has become legendary) plunged below $1 per share. The foundation for this collapse was set many quarters in advance. This event precipitated devastating losses for investors, mutual funds, and several state retirement funds.

Sadly, on the eve of this collapse, all the major investment houses were touting Enron stock and were still giving "buy" recommendations. This magnified the problem and further undermined the growing loss of confidence that investors have in stockbrokers and brokerage institutions.

In the aftermath of Enron, the plight of other major companies was brought to light, adding to the growing distress in the marketplace. Cases were brought against Merrill Lynch and most major Wall Street investment firms by the attorney general of New York State, Eliot Spitzer. These cases resulted in huge fines to these firms and mandated that they make public many of the practices that led to such great losses during the early years of this century.

In an article picked up by all the major news services, Arianna Huffington stated, "New York Attorney General Eliot Spitzer says Merrill Lynch, like Enron, intentionally peddled bad investments to boost its bottom line."[5]

(Eliot Spitzer was sworn in as New York's fifty-eighth governor on January 1, 2007. It would be a great education for any investor to go to www.google.com and enter Eliot Sptizer. You will be amazed at some of the things he exposed relative to Wall Street firms and the major brokerage houses. The number of companies fined and the amounts of their fines are mind-boggling.)

However, there was some good news on the horizon. Shortly after Enron's collapse, a small, unknown company named Stock-Diagnostics.com completed work on stock analysis software that provided an alternative to the previous methods of picking stocks. This software was based on algorithms and analysis using cash flow information identified in corporate quarterly and yearly reports. The development of this methodology goes back to the late 1970s and early 1980s, when some very successful Wall Street brokers began to investigate an alternative to the earnings per share (EPS) methodology of analyzing the strength of a stock.

The first project addressed by the new software was an autopsy of Enron to identify the cause of its collapse. An anomaly was discovered in the cash flow analysis that indicated several quarters in advance that Enron was in trouble. Using this information an investor could have been alerted; investors would have been advised to sell the stock at least several quarters in advance of the collapse of Enron. Thousands of small investors lost their entire personal retirement accounts in the Enron collapse because they just did not have good information; imagine what this new methodology could have meant to them.

After the autopsy on Enron, StockDiagnostics.com went back and looked at over three hundred companies that had gone bankrupt in the previous five years, including Sunbeam. It was found that they all shared the same anomaly!

When you read stock reports, hear bankers speak or experts interviewed on cable networks, you always hear them refer to Earnings Per Share (EPS). While EPS is certainly one factor to be weighed, it has become the mantra of Wall Street that everyone just accepts without understanding some of the flaws associated with EPS. There are a number of problems inherent in this analysis methodology, as proved by Enron and numerous other companies. The capability of masking information and inflating data is a proven fact and lies at the base of Eliot Spitzer's indictments of major Wall Street firms.

In the early years of the twenty-first century stock market scandal, greed and dishonesty pervaded companies such as Quest, Adelphia, Global Crossing, WorldCom, and others. All of these companies were under investigation for fraudulent accounting. The ability to manipulate information—coupled with incredible corruption—was at the root of the problem.

With respect to Global Crossing it was said, "The corporation, it appears, arranged deals in which no goods or services were exchanged, but nonetheless made it appear that profit was being generated."[6] These purely paper transactions inflated the company's revenue substantially. Take note that there was actually no cash flow generated from these transactions and yet the fraudulent reports caused many brokerage houses to give buy recommendations, resulting in huge losses to investors.

StockDiagnostics.com has coined a new term based on its algorithms and analysis. It is Operational Cash Flow Per Share (OPS). This term goes right to the strength of companies based on their available cash and cash flow. Companies that have strong OPS are more likely to succeed and be viable. Therefore, unlike EPS, which provides information after the fact, OPS is an indicator of the future strength of companies. Therefore a portfolio containing a diversity of stocks that have strong OPS should outperform any other stock-picking methodology that relies on EPS.

Warren Buffett and Barry Diller are two well-known investors whose acquisition of companies has created tremendous wealth for them and their shareholders. They have staff who routinely seek out cash flow information on public companies, and that information becomes the basis for their decision on whether to buy a company. Individual investors have not had access to such information. Now StockDiagnostics.com has found a way to make that information available to the average investor who wishes to achieve greater return on his or her stock portfolio. While StockDiagnostics.com is not a broker, it does provide the portfolio information to its subscribers that enables them to invest in portfolios selected by the OPS methodology. These portfolios have a proven track record of returns competitive with the S&P 500 and far outperforming most mutual funds.

By establishing a proprietary relationship with an online broker/dealer named FOLIOfn, subscribers to StockDiagnostics.com portfolio information may purchase their own portfolio with the ability to perform up to 400 trades per month for under $30 per month. FOLIOfn was founded in 1998 by Steve Wallman, a former commissioner of the Securities and Exchange Commission. It was announced in October 2005 that "the Pentagon has tapped Internet-based brokerage FOLIOfn Investments, Inc. to become its exclusive provider of online brokerage and investment services."[7] On October 17, 2005, the Pentagon Federal Credit Union announced that FOLIOfn would be its exclusive online brokerage provider. (Many other industry announcements were made throughout the mainstream and industry press. There should be no reason to list them all here as they are easily accessible to anyone interested in finding them.)

Red Herring (a weekly magazine focused on the business of funding, building, and taking new technologies to market) highlighted FOLIOfn in its May 2001 issue, placing the company on its annual list of the top 100 companies most likely to change the world, and stating "FOLIOfn's low pricing and innovative service could fundamentally change the mutual fund industry…"

FOLIOfn allows investors to establish an account online through a very easy-to-navigate system. An investor may start with and make contributions as small as $10 per order. The reason FOLIOfn is able to do this is because they've created a system that allows the company to sell fractional shares. In the case of StockDiagnostics.com portfolio recommendations, investors utilizing FOLIOfn can have their contribution spread over a diversified portfolio of one hundred or more stocks, the selection of which is based on OPS, with the click of a button. The investment contribution is spread evenly over the portfolio.

However, as stocks go up or down in value, the weighted average of the monies in a given stock may change in relation to other stocks. In the case of a typical mutual fund, the weighted average of stocks must be balanced because it is mandated by law that no one stock may have no more than 5 percent of the portfolio invested in it. But with FOLIOfn methodology, the investor has total access to view and/or change his portfolio selections. This means that he can choose to keep "winners." (As an example, if your portfolio were to contain the next Microsoft, how would you feel if it were sold off to keep the portfolio balanced?)

I don't mean to suggest that balancing the portfolio does not have some merit. It just means that you, as the investor, can have some input on where your money is invested. Based on updated recommendations regularly provided by StockDiagnostics.com, an investor is allowed to buy or sell any stocks in his portfolio. The good news is that since the stocks are selected based on OPS, the true cash flow strength of a company, changes will likely be minimal. But, when necessary, due to changes in OPS rankings, sell recommendations are issued.

The StockDiagnostics.com portfolios also allow you, the investor, to choose to retain or drop a particular stock due to your own preferences. You may have conscience- or business-related reasons that mandate you avoid certain stocks. It is your decision if you wish to remove a particular stock and insert another. For example, you may not wish to own shares in a company that manufacturers or distributes tobacco products. Or there may be other conflicts that you wish to avoid.

Whatever the reason for you to choose different stocks, you are provided numerous recommendations of companies with high OPS ranking. This flexibility alone may be reason enough to carefully examine the StockDiagnostics.com portfolios. As you investigate this option, you may find other good reasons that fit your needs. You may learn about FOLIOfn by going to their Web site: www.foliofn.com.

StockDiagnostics.com also markets its portfolios through TheRetirementSolution.com, which became a public company in September of 2006 and is presently being traded as a bulletin board stock under the symbol tres.ob. TheRetirementSolution.com subscribes to the notion of three pillars of strength when investing: intelligence, safety, and convenience. The company's Web site provides complete information describing how those pillars can be the foundation of a sound stock investment strategy. This will be a company to watch. It should come into view nationally during 2007 and 2008.

Out of all the business models I discuss in this book, there is one that has caught my attention. JGO Financial incorporates many of the financial solutions I recommend—but with a twist. If you are familiar with Amazon.com, then you may be familiar with "referral marketing" or "affiliate marketing." Amazon.com is just one of the twenty-first century business models that thrives by rewarding people for introducing others to its product or service. Internationally, the concept of receiving compensation for passing forward a product or service is truly a way of life.

In the last ten years throughout the United States the expectation of referral compensation has risen to new heights year after year. Some companies even provide two-level affiliate structures, where you can earn residual income from both the person you refer and from the person they refer. JGO Financial is one company that incorporates the sophistication of a financial education and information product with an opportunity to earn while you create a nest egg for your future.

Best-selling authors like David Bach and Robert Kiyosaki talk about how referral marketing is the most powerful and most efficient marketing medium on the planet today. Companies like JGO Financial (www.jgofinancial.com) capitalize on the success of referral marketing by providing all of the perks of a financial services product with the upside potential of a real home-business.

Think about it. If your retirement account is outperforming all other indices, chances are you are going to tell others about it. Traditionally, word-of-mouth compensation models have been used to promote products and/or services that created some type of positive emotional experience. JGO Financial takes this concept to the next level. With their education and information system, you now have concrete, undisputed results to provide to a potential member. Everyone is receiving valuable education and information. Subscribers can show their friends and family the exceptional past performance of their own retirement portfolios.

Speaking of earning extra money, the Cube compensation model provided by JGO Financial is noteworthy. They have the most fair, most lucrative compensation model I have ever seen. I interviewed Shawn Wheeland, the president and CEO of this company personally. He says, "At JGO Financial, we are dedicated to making sure that more money is built into our compensation plan for the people who deliver the message than for the corporation's bottom line. Of course, the company must be profitable to stay in business. However, I recognize the importance of the positive message that is delivered person to person. We are paying more money to the messenger than the company is keeping for profits. This creates a huge win-win scenario for the company."

Another positive is that JGO Financial has built their model around unique and proven portfolio offerings. This company allows you to do two things. First, you benefit firsthand by growing your own portfolio with stocks in companies that have strong cash and cash flow indicators (OPS). Second, as you gain personal experience with your own portfolio, you may determine that you would like to tell others. Wouldn't you tell your family and friends if you experienced safe returns in excess of mutual funds and other established benchmarks? The company will pay you for person-to-person advertising on their behalf.

If you are looking for a financial services product with a twist, JGO Financial is at least one company that is heading in the right direction. The past performance of their portfolios is well documented. Mr. Wheeland says that each investor can "earn a significant income by simply showing others how well [his] own portfolio is performing." Remember, it is your responsibility to create your own nest egg. This company provides you the opportunity to pass on this message of responsibility and turn it into a real business. As Mr. Wheeland points out, "You are probably already doing it. You are just not getting paid for it." You can read more at www.jgofinancial.com.

Are there other strategies and/or companies that offer alternatives that have merit? Indeed there are! There is a growing awareness of the need for investors to take more control of their investments and retirement planning. New companies are stepping forward to fill the information and education gap at a time when those concerned about their retirement need it the most.

For example, Investools says it offers education and information on how to make your own trades. Investools claims that it has trained over a quarter million Americans to utilize available information and take a measure of control over their investments. Their slogan is, "It is time to put your financial future in the best possible hands. Your own!" To learn more about Investools, go to NASDAQ and look for the stock symbol SWIM. Or access the company's Web site: www.investools.com.

Other sites that may provide valuable assistance to you include www.TDAMERITRADE.com, www.Scottrade.com, and www.themotleyfool.com. For a wide range of information, legal and otherwise, check out the Web site for the Securities and Exchange Commission at www.sec.gov.

Again, remember that you must establish the risk versus reward that gives you the most comfort; this cannot be determined as a formula for everyone across the board. You may not get rich with a certificate of deposit, but in the interest of diversification, most financial planners will advise you to place at least a portion of your assets in a CD or some other instrument with a guaranteed return. As you grow older you will likely place a much more conservative amount of your assets at risk in aggressive strategies. Baby boomers, however, demand more flexibility than any previous generation. We now understand that it is in our best interests to be fully involved in the management of our personal finances and our ongoing retirement planning.

* * *

How did I get to the point where I'd lost all that I had built up financially? I made the decision to really go after that last major project even though by now I was a multimillionaire and did not need it. But I had made many good decisions in the past and felt I knew what needed to be done. I convinced myself that I was making another good decision. After all, we had more than five hun-

dred employees and contractors on our projects at one point and there were several key people on payroll that were dependent upon me continuing the operation and growing the company even bigger.

So I no longer had control on where this was heading. I was now serving the interests of this separate entity that I had created. It was beginning to consume me. I was plunging headlong into disaster and had become a bystander unable to change the direction.

Finally, the contracts on this last project were signed. I had justified all the confidence placed in me by my employees, the banks, my insurance advisors and admirers. The project had been a dream of mine. I had the plan, the clients to occupy the property, and the desire to get it done. When the owner refused to sell the property to me, he suggested that I design and build it for *him. There were some warning signs and I felt that I did not have the complete picture of the person I was dealing with, but a couple of months of negotiations led to a comfort level that convinced me to proceed.*

From the start it became clear that I had bitten off more than I could chew. This was a cost-plus project, where we billed for the work in arrears. We started out with vigor and enthusiasm. But from the first we were faced with difficulty getting paid for the contracted work on this multimillion dollar project. Extracting my company at this point proved to be impossible.

Toward the end of the project, with unpaid bills to contractors and suppliers building, the client conveniently left the country for an extended period. I was left with the dilemma of either discontinuing the project until he returned and we were paid, or completing the project while I had all contractors committed and ready to finish. After much deliberation, I chose to continue.

When he finally returned we were nearly finished. I was anxious to be paid so I could compensate my subcontractors and suppliers who had stood by me through the project.

At last, we had a meeting with the client. I had my attorney with me. When confronted with all the remaining invoices, his cold, calculating voice penetrated straight through all the confidence and personal image that I had worked so hard to establish.

He simply said, "Sue me. I am not going to pay any more for this project." The trap had closed.

But I was not going to be so easily dismissed in that way. I proudly responded, "I will see you in court." I was not about to settle with that #@%&! Oh, I could have settled and would have lost plenty, but I would have still maintained my business.

The next three years were consumed by litigation, filled with discovery, lawyer's offices, and wasted effort. I tried to continue the business but when you are wrapped up in a suit such as this, it consumes your mind, your energy, and your time. I got the best lawyer from the best firm money could buy. He agreed when I said that "right is on my side." He assured me that we would not only win but would receive a judgment in excess of our claims.

As the time-consuming process continued, I reminded my attorney that right was on my side and that the truth had to win out. I will never forget his words to me when I was at my most desperate: "You keep confusing the truth with the law."

LESSON 11: Retreat, regroup, and supplicate.

What did I learn from the foregoing experience? It seems clear to me that we should exhaust every means possible to try and more fully understand the position of an adversary. We should as accurately as possible determine whether there are options to resolve the conflict that were not seen in the heat of battle. I say *heat of battle* because it became obvious to me that my skilled client had pushed the right buttons that made me be reactive rather than proactive. To tell an experienced attorney that you will see him in court is, on the face of it, simply ludicrous. But he so maneuvered me that I became righteously indignant. Years later, that seems so silly of me.

I could not have made his job easier. He had the situation in his control and I was led along to the point of exhaustion and exasperation. You cannot make good, responsible decisions when you are in that frame of mind.

Another lesson that manifested itself is that the justice system can be less than just to the unprepared and ill-informed. The all-consuming discovery process is confusing and troubling. Sleepless nights filled with worry while trying to sort out how to keep a company afloat, caring for the needs of employees and vendors while spending seemingly endless hours in the discovery process, proved to be debilitating and more than a little stressful.

The lesson from this should be to first follow your instincts about whom you do business with. If there are warning signs, move on to the next potential deal or client. When confronted with a belligerent, dominating adversary, remove yourself from the situation for a sufficient period of time to make clear judgments and decisions. Seek to find a way for reconciliation. Once you clearly understand what your adversary is after, determine what you can give up in the short term that will allow you long-term relief. As the proverb says, "It is better to be a live dog than a dead lion."

This may mean begging your adversary for relief. This may take more courage than choosing to risk everything by jumping into the fight. To make it palatable, let's call it *supplicate your adversary*. Today I would say to an adversary, "Help me understand what it is that you are looking for and let's see how we can make this a win-win situation."

* * *

Based on my attorney's assurances, we tried to continue the business. We used our cash reserves and then began to liquidate properties to pay off the contractors and suppliers. I am thankful that we were able to care for all or most of them by using up our resources. Those admirers began to distant themselves. My friends would walk by and I could feel them shaking their head as they went past me.

Working very hard, I was able to avoid personal bankruptcy. And because of the good reputation I had built up with our bankers, I was able to preserve my personal credit. I will never forget the wonderful creditors and others who worked with me during this most desperate of times.

You see, my wife and I did not believe in bankruptcy and did not know anyone in our family or in our association who had ever gone bankrupt. So we were determined to avoid that course, although it could have preserved some of our assets.

LESSON 12: A bankruptcy moves in and lives with you for a very long time.

I still do not advocate bankruptcy. It is true that it is a legal and important tool that some may be forced to employ, and as I've said, might preserve an important asset such as a home. But there are often years-long consequences that prove to be just as difficult as the previous circumstance. As one boomer who said he was forced into bankruptcy told me, "I got out of the frying pan into the fire." In his case, he said that it would have been better to liquidate all his assets and work his way through the situation.

There are other options that an attorney and/or consumer counseling service could point you to that deserve consideration before bankruptcy. Be sure to consider some of these options. In spite of the events that overtook me and my family because of my decision to take on that last project, I am still glad that I did not file for bankruptcy.

* * *

After more than three years, we finally got the client to court in front of the judge we had hoped for. As we got into the court that Monday morning, my attorney urged us to wait while he and the client went into the judge's quarters for a conference. When he came out he told me that the client had agreed to pay all that was owed less any damages or attorney's fees. My attorney told me not to worry about his unpaid fees. We could work through that later. He said that all that needed to be done was to have the agreement drawn up and on Friday we could sign it and be paid. The deadline passed and the client never signed the agreement. He just thumbed his nose at us and dared us to continue the lawsuit. He won because he knew that we wanted peaceful resolution. He had calculated that he could outlast us and that he did.

The irony of this entire situation is that it could have been avoided by simply passing on that last project. It would have meant making some adjustments, but they would not have been as catastrophic as the agony that our family went through because I chose to take on this project. The writer of the song "The Gambler" really had it close to right when he said, "You have to know when to hold them ... and know when to fold them." Isn't it amazing how much sense these words seem to make—especially in business?

Another reason that I took on this last project is because a number of my friends' livelihoods were tied up with the success of the company and my efforts. I have never been bottom-line oriented. I was concerned about those employees and that weighed heavily on my mind.

At that time the stock market was about to take off on its historic rise through the next ten to fifteen years. Dad's words that I would never have had to work again would have come true.

LESSON 13: Life is a journey, not a destination.

There are consequences to all of our decisions even if they are thrust upon us. When I made the conscious decision to put the past behind me I began to have hope again. I realized that I could only control what I do and not anyone else. Like never before, I took responsibility for my decisions and chose not to blame them on anyone else. I very quickly began to heal when I came to that realization.

Sadly, it took several years for that to happen. We were in the midst of cleaning up the incredible mess that closing our business and liquidating properties created. We finally just decided to accept our lumps—our losses. That opened a new, exciting and rewarding chapter in our lives. It is one that, with little or with much, we will approach with hope and enthusiasm. The joy of living has some pain with it but how sweet it is to wake each day excited about its unique prospects.

* * *

One very important thing to realize is that at this point in my life I never thought that I would live to retirement age. I say this because I remember a life insurance agent, who was a fellow pilot, told me when I was thirty-one years of age that due to the pace of life I lived, I would likely not see forty (what a great salesman, huh?). And I felt that I would need to keep working for another ten to fifteen years. The idea of liquidating assets and living off them seemed unreasonable. That is only because I was not really thinking in terms of simplifying my life. It is only looking back that I realize what a sea change of thinking that requires.

That was the last time I ever got close to settling with the client or getting him to court. At this point I simply gave up, accepted my losses and decided to go on with my life. The attorneys had cost hundreds of thousands of dollars, I no longer had a business, my employees had either gone elsewhere or I had helped set them up in their own businesses. My wife and I had liquidated almost all of our assets.

As I look back from the perspective of over fifteen years, I realize that I truly did go beyond a formal education. This education and experience cost me everything I had built up in nearly twenty-five years. Although the lingering painfulness of the experience will never go away, there has been a mellowing over the years that has provided perspective that I could never have achieved any other way.

We used to laugh (to keep from crying) because losing several million dollars has caused some people to jump out their office windows. I'm thankful that I had the good sense to place my office on the ground floor when we built our office building!

During all of this time period, I had not been solely focused on business and making money. In fact, I viewed my business and its success as the vehicle that allowed me to continue to be very involved in volunteer work. For most of this time I served as chairman of a charitable organization that provided construction services for religious meeting places throughout the southeast United States, Bermuda, and the Caribbean islands. During 1990, our group had the privilege to assist in sharing ideas and training other groups in Germany, Switzerland, and France.

When Hurricane Hugo hit Charleston, South Carolina, in September 1989, we were among the first groups on the scene the next day with money, materials, and manpower. We had the privilege of helping provide shelter for hundreds of people dispossessed or needing a helping hand. But the devastation of that last project threw me off track so much that I had to resign from those privileged responsibilities that I loved so much.

There is still more to learn. I'm sure life has more lessons for me. I do not consider myself unique, but different only in the particulars of the circumstances. Over the last fifteen years I have learned that many baby boomers share a similar history. We often jokingly say, "There are only two kinds of people. The ones that have gone through an experience like I have and the ones that are going to."

The truth is, not everyone has or will go through those experiences. But it highlights the fact that such experiences are, anecdotally speaking, a very significant part of the passage of many baby boomers.

LESSON 14: Should you be fired?

There is another huge lesson that I learned through this experience. When it comes to managing money, there may come a time when we have to fire ourselves. We may have to admit that we need advice and guidance from an expert. But even that may have its pitfalls, as you have seen.

On September 24, 2007, *USA Today* ran an article titled, "Pros Fess Up to Their Retirement-Building Blunders." Mark Zandi, chief economist at Moody's Economy.com stated that his biggest mistake was "letting savings languish." He said, "I don't think many of us get any kind of formal training in personal finance. At least I didn't. The only training I got was that I watched my father do the bills." Zandi said the experience taught him the importance of educating his three children about investing. We agree when he says, "Managing your personal finances is a daily affair. It's like brushing your teeth."

Several other renowned "experts" were quoted in this article and all of them confessed to various things they should have done differently. Some others quoted included: Sheryl Garrett, founder of Garrett Planning Network (a network of fee-only financial planners for middle-income consumers); Tom Gardner, cofounder and CEO of The Motley Fool (an investment advice Web site); and Robert Willens, managing director, tax and accounting expert at Lehman Bros. Among the blunders were "overconfidence" and "began saving too late." All this from people who, like you and I, could have done a better job at some point in managing their resources and their PRA.

When I realized how badly I had managed my PRA, I fired myself. However, I've learned from that precipitous firing. Over the years I made it my business to gain knowledge of investments and an understanding of how money works. This has led to increased confidence—to the point where I felt I could rehire myself. After all, no one wishes for my investments to be successful as much as I do!

* * *

Looking for a little more help? Other sources of advice are available on the Internet. There are many Web sites that offer financial and retirement information. There is often a cost to accessing this information, but it may be useful as you do your personal research. For example:

- mPower, an Internet-based investment advisory service, offers its mPower Café 401(k) page at www.mpower.com.
- www.quicken.com includes a retirement section.
- T. Rowe Price and Morningstar Associates have teamed up to offer free online financial planning advice to 401(k) participants.
- www.financialengines.com offers its advisory service on employee retirement plans, including 401(k) plans, free to Vanguard clients.
- www.selectaretirementplan.org is provided by the combined efforts of the Department of Labor, the Small Business Administration, the Chamber of Commerce, and Merrill Lynch & Co.

- www.choosetosave.org was developed by the American Savings Education Council and the Employee Benefits Research Institute. There is also a "Ballpark Estimate" retirement planning worksheet available at www.asec.org.

The Experts /
Failed Opinions

*I*n many ways the early 1990s were sad years. I felt that I had lost track of some of my identity. Having lost millions—a fortune surpassing that of any of my family—I felt like a failure financially. I had lost my confidence about my ability to manage a successful business. I was not sure that I could regroup and start over.

Within three years we relocated to Atlanta, Georgia. Atlanta is the financial center of the South, and I knew that I could recover financially there in a big arena. The dealings with our old company were complete now. There was only one thing to do and that was to start over.

Coming out of this dark period, I felt the thing to do was start over from the bottom. Ironically, I started another small janitorial business and my son worked with me when he could.

The founder of a major manufacturing company in the industry from North Carolina knew of my history, as we had become friends over the years. His company was now about twenty-five years old and the darling of its industry worldwide, with both domestic and foreign distributors. He invited me to come to the home office in North Carolina. Not knowing what he had in mind, I left Atlanta early one morning for the four hour drive, after first saying a prayer with my wife, because we frankly did not know how we would pay the next month's rent.

Our meetings went very well. Not only did he offer me a consulting position with the company as his personal envoy to the company's distributors, he also sensed my desperation, although I had not said a thing about our financial plight. He asked me if an advance would be helpful because it would be a couple of weeks before our agreement would start. I told him that would be appreciated, thinking he might give me something like a $500 advance. He called the CFO but I could not hear what he told him. When the CFO came into the president's office he handed me a check that I was afraid to look at. I thanked them, and made arrangements to keep in touch and be back in two weeks for instructions.

Can you imagine my emotions, excitement, relief, and appreciation when I got to my car and looked at a $5,000 advance check? There was no turning back now. My recovery was well on the way. This time our prayer was one of thankfulness, and a request that we not ever forget to recognize where good things come from. Often it is not our own merit or initiative that saves us, but the blessing of God and good friends.

Not only did I have an advance, but also a substantial income and health benefits. I was going to be traveling all over North America calling on distributors, and soon my responsibilities included calling on and consulting with virtually every major chain in the United States, Canada, and Mexico.

What a joy it was to go from the pits of depression to calling on the corporate offices of Sears, Target, Wal-Mart, Kroger, Albertson's, Walgreens, Rite Aid, and many others. I now had the privilege to expand my education while meeting with many fellow baby boomers at the highest levels of business and industry. I found that a number of them had stories similar to mine. Representing the company, I had the honor of playing in numerous charity golf tournaments, often teaming up with board members and officers of major corporations. I got to know these leaders in formal and informal settings.

When I was able to successfully complete a major contract with Wal-Mart, the president of my company and I were photographed together at Wal-Mart with their executives at the signing of the agreement. That was the feature article in Wal-Mart's next company newsletter.

My income had now increased to the point where we could buy a new home near Lake Lanier, north of Atlanta. We had begun to build our financial reserves again.

Although the stock market was continuing to grow, I still didn't know anyone I trusted to give me good advice. And after all, I needed to keep my cash reserves available in banks in case I had urgent need. What did I need the stock market for? With all my interest and desire to be informed about different fields, I still had this gaping void where anything to do with the stock market was concerned. I continued to view the stock market as if it were gambling. Clearly, the biggest gamble I had taken had been with my own company. Things were improving so I just continued to go with the flow.

My company was sold to the Japanese and my friend, the president, chose not renew his contract but to retire. He told me there would be great changes. The Japanese no longer wanted just market share, they now wanted profits. He felt that there would be a number of longtime employees released upon his departure, but that my value to the company was great and I would likely not be one of them. Nonetheless, to be safe, he offered me a one-year severance that included keeping my health insurance benefits in effect during that time, to allow me to move into something else if I so desired. I chose to accept; approving my severance proved to be the president's last official act.

LESSON 15: Learn to recognize when it's time to move on.

One of the most difficult things to do is to leave a situation that we are familiar with and venture out into the unknown. That is especially difficult to do when you are at the top of your game or profession.

Many years ago a banker wished to go into the real estate industry. He toyed with the idea for a long time. He knew me when I closed out a very successful business and moved into an entirely new industry with great success. Later, after he became one of the most successful realtors in Asheville, North Carolina, he told me that what I did gave him the courage to follow his heart. He never looked back and never regretted leaving the banking industry.

Over the years I only stayed in an industry and/or line of work as long as it excited me and I enjoyed it. Another guiding principle was that I continued to place a high premium on having the freedom to arrange my own schedule. My passion for writing this book has driven me for several years. I did not get serious until I resigned as president/CEO of a company and then turned down a great offer of employment.

That may lead you to believe that I don't have to work. Not true. But rather than be subject to the dictates of a boss, I have chosen to take on various consulting contracts so that I could maintain control of my own schedule. This has also opened time for me to engage in more volunteer work and has given me the freedom to devote even more time to managing my own PRA.

Several years ago when I was experiencing one of the downturns in the mortgage banking industry, I was given the book *Who Moved My Cheese?* It is a little book but put in perspective what I am trying to convey to you here. There are times when it is simply time to move on. Sometimes it is thrust upon us and we have no choice but to go.

Whatever the reasons for moving on, we should recognize that due to our age and experience many baby boomers have a lot to offer and will for a long time to come. I will never forget the story of the maintenance supervisor in the large regional hospital in my hometown. He had been a customer of mine for several years, so I knew him quite well. He knew every knob and switch in that hospital. In time the new administration decided that they needed to build a huge new addition to the hospital. They built the addition without tearing down or upgrading the old section of the hospital.

To facilitate the new addition the hospital hired, at great expense, a newly minted engineer unfamiliar with the hospital. Of course, they persuaded the old maintenance supervisor to take an early retirement. It wasn't long before the new engineer began to experience problems. It seems the only person who knew enough about the systems to correct the problems was the old maintenance supervisor.

You guessed it—the old maintenance supervisor, now retired, has become a consultant. Yes, the hospital hired him back, but as a consultant he makes considerably more than he did as an employee. And now he has control of his own schedule and can exercise the freedom of when to come and go.

Is it time for you to go? There are so many opportunities where the skills, experience and foresight of baby boomers have great value. Your talents are needed as never before. You have every reason to believe that your best years are now.

* * *

During the next year, several opportunities presented themselves. I had built a very successful network marketing organization in the travel industry in less than one year. It culminated in hosting nearly 2,000 agents in Atlanta; the city even declared a day for that company, based on my efforts working with the Greater Atlanta Chamber of Commerce. We had numerous prestigious celebrities, Miss Georgia, a state senator, and a representative of the city to present a key to the city to the chairman of the travel company.

Changed circumstances with that company paved the way for me to accept the recruiting efforts of a company from Nashville, Tennessee. I was recruited and hired as their national sales manager and relocated to Nashville in 1998.

Prior to this, in 1996, I had developed a close friendship with a gentleman who happened to be a very successful financial planner who had all the securities licenses. His impressive offices were located in one of the beautiful Atlanta skyscrapers. As our friendship grew I gradually began to learn from him about mutual funds but I didn't do my own research. I just relied on his experience and obvious knowledge of the industry. I trusted him. He had many clients that he introduced me to and I golfed with some of them. They were very pleased with his work on their behalf. He is a man of integrity and I still respect him and consider him a friend, in spite of the events that followed.

Shortly after having completed my move to Nashville, I contacted my financial planner friend in Atlanta to inquire about dis-

cussing my portfolio and having him manage at least some of my financial assets. They had not grown to the previous level I had enjoyed ten years prior but they were beginning to build up again. This time I was not going to take a chance. I was going to work with a professional and make sure that I diversified.

After several meetings I began to feel that perhaps I might wind up with a retirement nest egg after all. My wife and I decided to invest approximately 50 percent of our newly acquired assets with our friend. We still held back due to our apprehension and still having only a vague understanding of the markets and mutual funds.

I clearly remember my friend telling me that once we invested in mutual funds, we should be in them for the long haul. He said we should forget about that money and let the compounding of interest take care of itself. I still had not been told or taught about the Rule of 72.

LESSON 16: Learn the Rule of 72.

The Rule of 72 is a formula that simply states the time required for money to double at a given rate of interest, by dividing 72 by the interest rate. For example, 72 divided by a 6 percent rate of interest means that a given amount of money earning that 6 percent will double in twelve years. Similarly, a given amount of money earning 12 percent will double in six years.

Clearly, years lost when savings or investments might have been growing cannot be recaptured. However, you can still achieve many of your goals by either increasing the amount of your contributions into savings or by obtaining a greater return on your savings and/or investments. (How did I miss this in my education? I guess the same way most other baby boomers did. We were not taught it at any point in school and the bankers sure aren't going to teach it to us.)

* * *

For the next few years I just forgot about those funds, except that we continued to make contributions to our Simple 401(k) plan. Af-

ter the dot-com debacle and the adjustments that followed, however, I thought I'd better go see my friend and find out what had happened with my investments.

Driving into downtown Atlanta, I felt a growing concern that I was not going to hear good news. But after all, this was my good friend and surely he had watched over and shepherded my investments, knowing that this was our retirement he had in his hands. So I decided I would be optimistic and expect the best.

As I rode the elevator up to his high rise offices my spirits were rising too. It was over ten years since the devastating events in North Carolina. I had already had two successful careers since being in Atlanta. I had a good position with a rapidly growing company in the financial services industry. My current income was good. We had a new house in Tennessee. Our son had moved to New York to do volunteer work.

To top things off, when I walked into his office my friend was upbeat and top o' the morning. My concerns seemed to be unnecessary. We talked for some time about what had happened in the stock market and how the mutual funds had taken a beating.

Through our entire discussion he continued to be his usual charming and happy self. By now, comfortable in the big, plush chair, looking out at traffic zooming by on one of the connectors, I forgot about being anxious with respect to my investments.

After some time my friend suggested that we review my portfolio. He got up, walked behind his desk and pulled up my portfolio information on his screen. I patiently waited while he looked over everything and then came to the edge of my chair when he was ready to tell me how much my investments had earned.

He said, "Good news!" All right—just what I wanted to hear. Remember, my neighbor on the mountain in North Carolina, the stockbroker. Recall how her answer made such an impression. What I was about to hear proved to be "déjà vue all over again," as the saying goes. My friend continued, "Overall, the market has lost over 38 percent. Your portfolio has only lost about 30 percent."

Now, I don't pretend to be the greatest mathematician in the world. But I had no trouble figuring out what that meant. Immedi-

ately, I realized that I had not only lost a major portion of my investments. I now knew about the Rule of 72 (see Appendix B). I fully understood now what it meant to lose that time when my earnings could have been compounding.

At that point I looked him in the eye and said, "You're fired!"

He said, "You can't fire me. I'm your friend."

I said, "You're still my friend ... you're still fired!"

The Search Continues

I *still had my position in Tennessee and was earning excellent income. My new company was in the residential mortgage industry, established as a correspondent lender doing business throughout the US. Back working in the mortgage industry again, I immersed myself in making a success of that opportunity. My responsibilities included recruiting, hiring, and training account executives to develop mortgage broker clients. The company was extremely successful and by 1999 became an acquisition target.*

Seeing the handwriting on the wall, I gave my notice and with a partner established a new mortgage company. This company eventually was licensed in over thirty states working with a number of major banks nationwide, doing correspondent lending, working with our own money and warehouse lines, underwriting, processing, packaging, and selling mortgage loans on the secondary market. At the height of this business we had approximately sixty on payroll.

By 2002 we had established a client base and reputation such that I was invited to educate consumers on the highest-rated locally produced television program in the Nashville market. When first asked to participate, I asked if the producers were sure that their viewers would watch a thirty-minute program dedicated to residential mortgage information. They assured me that it was the most requested subject of their viewers at that time.

After rehearsing the program, I arrived at the studio at the appointed time for the taping, wearing a banker's three-piece striped blue suit with a red tie. The interviewer, who was also a client of mine, said, "Take off that tie. You are no tied-assed banker." I did and we produced the number-one rated program for that season. The program had so many requests for re-airing that it was replayed on the station's cable channel many times that season. A number of CPAs, financial planners, and others from the financial industry called to inquire about the program, to congratulate us, and some became our clients or referred clients to our company.

One of the things that made the program so successful was that I was introducing financial concepts that were generally unknown in the marketplace and to this day are still largely misunderstood. I was explaining to viewers that consumers should view their home mortgage as an integral part of their financial planning and that it could become a wealth-building tool for them. Early on I could only identify about twenty to twenty-five professionals nationwide advocating some of these principles. As time went by, many financial planners, mortgage professionals, and others began to realize the merit in more carefully analyzing the impact of the home mortgage on consumer wealth. Many consumers got the point, and along with other educators around the country, these concepts and programs accounted for approximately 30 percent of all new mortgages nationwide in recent years.

LESSON 17: Your home mortgage can be a powerful wealth-building asset.

Some of these strategies will have the potential to affect your retirement in a positive manner. I learned these lessons by careful observation. I discovered the companies highlighted here by working to manage my own PRA.

Your home mortgage is perhaps the area of greatest investment and greatest opportunity for you to maximize your financial resources. For example, for decades most consumers have been taught by bankers and advisors that the wisest course is to acquire a thirty-year fixed-rate mortgage. For decades after World War II there were very few other options available. So it is no wonder that strong paradigms exist.

Take careful note of the following statement. Your home mortgage can be your greatest liability or your greatest asset. Your goal is to be a wise, informed manager of your PRA. Always get the advice of your financial planner. But remember, many of the "experts" only point to the perils of new strategies. They often fail to point out the benefits to many investors and consumers. From personal experience, I can assure you that many of the experts do not believe that you and I are capable of managing our own resources. They fail to acknowledge that many baby boomers are better educated, better informed, and have access to enormous amounts of information.

As I am writing this, the media is filled with negative news regarding the sub-prime mortgage industry. Like many media-driven stories, the complete story is often buried under sensational reporting. The following information is not about the sub-prime mortgage industry. It has to do with providing competent individuals additional information that has proven to be extremely valuable to many who wish to exercise control over their financial future. As has been repeatedly stated, this book is about expanding your understanding and taking a measure of control over your own financial matters.

Bankers, stockbrokers, and corporate gurus have proven time and again that they are just as capable as any investor of making bad decisions and falling victim to models that time and again prove suspect. Increasingly, consumers are firing these so-called experts.

Would you not expect that the marketplace would naturally force companies to create new products and strategies? The experts who already feel they have it made frequently are unwilling to give new strategies the time of day. It is easier to sit back and arrogantly pronounce any new approach as too good to be true. Just because that statement is true some of the time does not mean that it is true all of the time.

In addition to that, there is the ever-present possibility of being victimized by a system motivated by greed. A recent Associated

Press article explained that due to accounting fraud, Fannie Mae agreed to a record 400 million dollar settlement. It said, "The accounting scandal that erupted in September 2004 brought the ouster of top executives at government sponsored Fannie Mae, which finances one of every five home loans in the United States. The company paid a record $400 million civil fine in a settlement last year of federal regulators' allegations of a pervasive six-year accounting fraud. *The scheme included accounting manipulations to reach Wall Street earnings targets so that Fannie Mae executives could pocket hundreds of millions in bonuses* from 1998–2004, the regulators said"[8] (emphasis mine).

Just think, some of these same executives and other experts have the temerity and the audacity to suggest that the average investor cannot make good, sound financial decisions. The truth is millions of baby boomers are awakening to the fact that they must be involved with the management of their financial affairs. This is too important a matter to leave solely in the hands of greedy managers who only view you as the stepping-stone to realizing their own financial goals.

The reasons for examining other, creative, innovative strategies should be clear. Therefore, the next questions are important. Is a thirty-year fixed-rate mortgage the best course for everyone? Are there other strategies that have merit and are worthy of consideration? In his bestseller "Ordinary People—Extraordinary Wealth," Ric Edelman lists eight major ways that ordinary people accumulate wealth. Edelman is recognized as one of the most successful financial advisors in America.

The first is "they carry a mortgage on their homes even though they can afford to pay it off."[9] Edelman explains this in his first chapter, "Why People Fear Mortgages and Why You Shouldn't." Did you know that many of our concepts and beliefs today are still based on the stock market crash of 1929? Edelman explains the changed conditions that allow investors and baby boomers a different approach than just following the dictates of the banking system. The banking system has its own vested interests that have to do with return on investment (ROI). It is not primarily concerned with optional strategies that may work better for many investors.

Edelman's conclusions are based on the evidence available through interviews and analysis of the financial situation of over 5,000 ordinary consumers. One thing common among all of them is that they keep large mortgages and view their mortgage as an integral part of their financial planning. There are many testimonials in his book that demonstrate the power of the strategies that are recommended. Edelman believes that "carrying a mortgage doesn't cause you to lose any money at all. In fact, just the opposite is true: carrying a mortgage is actually quite profitable. It's eliminating the mortgage that forces you to give up profitable opportunities. ... If you have a mortgage and you're dreaming of the day when you make your final payment, you're trying to do something that financially successful people do not do."[10] (You can access more specific information at: www.ricedelman.com.)

You can also refer to Appendix C for more detailed information on a variety of different mortgages. While determining which loan is right for you, there are some other things you should be informed about, and much information can be found on the Internet. Most lenders will have either a frequently asked questions (FAQs) section or they will have specific pages dedicated to these subjects. A few of the questions you will want to research include:

- Should I pay points?
- Does a zero-point/zero-fee loan really exist?
- What are the benefits and disadvantages of a zero-point/zero-fee loan?
- Whatever happened to the conventional wisdom of waiting for the rates to drop 2 percent before refinancing?
- What is a FICO score?
- What is a rate lock?
- Why do interest rates change?
- What is PMI? Can I get rid of PMI on my loan?

Is it really worthwhile to spend time researching this information? It is if you wish to be an educated consumer and you want to reduce your upfront and continuing monthly costs. Researching amortization, for example, could significantly impact your personal retirement account in a positive way. Refer to Appendix D for a detailed example and amortization chart.

* * *

Shortly after this, I learned of a networking company that had, independent of me, seized upon some of the concepts that I was propounding and was in the early stages of getting its message out. The principals of the company have a long track record in network marketing and in the financial services industry. After investigation it appeared that by working with this company I could get the message out to a larger audience and in some ways complement my core business.

The next year was an incredible ride. Soon after signing up, two gentlemen and I produced a one-hour video that eventually spread throughout the country. It summarized some of the benefits of those concepts that I had been promoting. Our organization began to grow. In the first six months, I was the top producer in the company, associated with the fastest growing organization in that company. In ten months our team recruited and initiated training for over 2,700 associates. We produced tens of millions in new business and won every award the company had to offer. In Las Vegas in 2003, my sponsor and I won every major award plus an all-expenses-paid trip to Hawaii for our spouses and us.

With my core business continuing and the successes of the networking company, I was multitasking with the best. I continued to feel that the networking success was compatible with my mortgage business. Having reviewed things with my attorney and those of the networking company, we felt that there was no conflict of interest.

This success sadly evaporated as the company began to focus on other expansion and could not, at that time, provide the support necessary to care for the huge volume of new business. For months, other mortgage industry professionals and I tried to provide the training support and guidance necessary to continue, but our organizations were floundering. The company was in its early stages. Under its new corporate name, Global Equity Lending now services a market that has allowed many of its associates to be-

come successful. According to Jeff Miles, one of the company's top leaders, "Global Equity Lending continues to seek out and promote cutting edge mortgage and financial services options." Mr. Miles made this statement in a telephone conversation with me in June, 2007.

After just one year, I resigned so that I could fully turn my attention to my core business. Since that time, the company has matured in the mortgage industry and has improved the management of the back office side of the industry. They are continuing to grow the business and many who stayed with the company have done well. It was also necessary for me to leave because, as a mortgage company owner and loan originator, I could not work for two companies. The laws respecting that have gotten progressively more restrictive.

For several years various banks approached me about acquiring my mortgage company. AmSouth Bank and Tennessee Bank & Trust were among some of those banks. SunTrust Bank hosted me at their corporate headquarters and operations offices. It looked like a good thing for me but meant leaving my team behind. My son had come into the business and, starting at the data entry level, he learned the business from the ground up. I am proud to say that he has proven to be an excellent mortgage loan officer and he now operates his own mortgage loan broker operation. Other banks made inquiries but the timing was never right and I did not want to leave my partner or my son.

In October of 2004, I experienced what my cardiologist called a "bell-ringer event." The doctor described it as a precursor to a massive heart attack. The most critical period is the first thirty minutes, and my son got me to the hospital within fifteen minutes of the onset of severe symptoms. This event resulted in a week's hospital stay and treatment. The good news was that there was no permanent damage to my heart and I could likely care for myself through diet and exercise. Even though I have not told you the entire story of my life you can probably see why the doctor could say that this event was caused by a build-up of stress.

During a month of recuperation, my company's own bank made a run at my company, hiring away some of my key people. In *fairness to those people, it is understandable that they could not be sure of my future, and I could never hold anything against them for accepting tempting offers that I could not have matched.*

When Branch Banking & Trust (BB&T) came calling early in 2005, I was a prime candidate. After much consideration and the family reaching agreement, I accepted their offer to close down my company and go to work for the bank. This major bank was moving strongly into the Middle Tennessee market and they were intent on creating a residential mortgage presence ahead of establishing branches. Because of what they called my standing in the community, I was offered a position as vice president with the bank.

For five years prior to coming into the bank I had traveled from one end of the country to the other meeting, attending seminars, and interviewing some of the most successful CPAs, financial planners, and business leaders. I attended their seminars and read their books. But until recent years, I still did not see the entire picture or understand what I needed to do to accomplish two things: create a retirement for myself, and discover a vehicle to educate my fellow baby boomers so that they, too, can create a retirement sufficient to care for their needs.

What you hold in your hand is that vehicle. I wish you, now, a long and fulfilling life, and a happy and comfortable retirement.

Boomers Seek Balance

T he thrust of this book has been about the baby boomers' efforts to create and manage financial wealth. However, as boomers have progressed in life and allowed life's lessons to set in, they have come to appreciate that a rewarding, fulfilling life is most often the result of having achieved some balance. With the financial pressures placed upon many today and the incredible assault of the marketing media, achieving balance often proves to be an elusive goal. Here are just a few final lessons I have learned that may prove useful to you. They are based on eternal principles that never change.

LESSON 18: Relationships are far more important than money.

Baby boomers have learned the hard way that money easily acquired is often more easily lost. While we place importance and value on managing our resources in a responsible way, we recognize that, at best, our authority over financial assets is temporary. We would, of course, like to provide some financial assurance to our mates as our capacity to provide income diminishes. We are all in danger of being exposed to unexpected challenges that are a threat to whatever assets we may have accumulated.

Since World War II, with the shift of population in this country and the movement of families away from one another, relationships with friends and family have been stretched to the breaking point. Sometimes families and close friends are apart for long periods of time. They become strangers to one another.

If we become preoccupied with acquiring and securing assets during all of our productive years, we stand the risk of alienating many of the relationships that are our real treasure. It goes without saying that a relationship with God has often been cast aside in the quest for riches. Can we say that this has made us a better, more compassionate people? Without the balance and benefit of godly direction, we may go through life with no real purpose.

Familial relationships are to be highly valued. Many baby boomers have told me that they regret that they spent so many years caught up in the pursuit of material things and money and they all but lost their families. Many did lose their families and are only now beginning to experience the sad heartache of lonely retirement years.

If our friendships are based on money and status, they will quickly disappear if our circumstances change for the worse. In fact, there is an adage that teaches us that to be wealthy we must stay around wealthy people. This presupposes that the only source of wealth is money and material things.

Everything of value has a price. The price of friendship is that we must be willing to put forth the time and effort to communicate by action that a relationship is important. The truth is that if want to have the best of friends, we must be a friend ourselves. We must give of ourselves for others. That means carving out the time to cultivate relationships. This, too, is accumulating wealth but of a more enduring kind.

LESSON 19: Never give up the quest for knowledge and understanding.

How many times can I emphasize this lesson? Baby boomers no longer just sit under the shade tree or on the front porch watching life go by. They are engaged and fascinated with all that goes on around them. I also call this generation the curious generation, or the generation that constantly searches for answers.

There is no end to the exciting or interesting things that we can learn. Never have we had so much access. We can explore the globe, outer space, and the depths of the seas through the power of the Internet. True, there are many negative things that are available on the Internet as well. But as more and more baby boomers gain confidence in the Internet and in the use of this tool, they will unleash all their experience and wisdom in pioneering new and different strategies.

Even if you don't have a computer or you are not yet proficient in utilizing the computer, there is much that you can do. You can check out your local community college or university for distance learning classes. It may be easier than you think to gain access. Even my eighty-four-year-old mother-in-law began to use the Internet and e-mail in the last five years.

Check out demonstrations at local computer stores. Use the computers at your public library. It has become very easy to buy a basic computer and obtain Internet service. Talk to your children and grandchildren. Today, even preschool children have had some exposure to the computer and many are advanced in its use. You may be surprised how delighted they would be to show you around.

Neither the computer nor the Internet need be scary. And for those of us who wish for knowledge and understanding, there is no limit to what we may learn. Do you want to learn to play a musical instrument? Do you want to travel and learn about cultures? Do you want to learn a new skill? All of this and more is available to us and we don't even have to leave home. Our lives can be like a good book with no ending.

LESSON 20: Growing older can be an adventure if we maintain a positive attitude.

The potential for some of us to experience a health issue or devastating circumstance is great. And we all, at some point, have to deal with old age and death. The truly distinguishing difference that I have seen in people is how we cope with those most difficult of life's trials.

During the writing of this book, my dear father died on October 1, 2006. He had survived colon cancer and was pronounced cancer-free in the fall of 2005. In the spring of 2006 he was diagnosed with lung cancer. Dad had quit smoking over forty years ago, but the doctor said smoking killed him.

In the spring of 2006 before the diagnosis, Dad said he felt the best he had in years. He was back to walking several miles a day. I'd rejoice when he would tell me in a phone conversation, "I am going to visit my old people today." He had just turned eight-eight. Dad said it looked like he was going to make ninety after all.

But from the time he was diagnosed with lung cancer and began chemotherapy and radiation, his situation steadily went downhill. He continued to drive until early summer of 2006 but by July it was obvious that he did not have long to live. He went into the hospital the middle of September 2006 and never came out.

During all of his illnesses and during the end of life period, Dad always impressed everyone with his good humor, his appreciation of little kindnesses, and his joy at making other people laugh. He was the epitome of a person with a good attitude.

Dad had great faith and confidence in the Bible's sure hope for the future. He eagerly looked forward to the resurrection that the Bible teaches. Without any sense of morbidity, Dad encouraged each of his sons to be worthy of being there to greet him and Mom in the resurrection. I am convinced that this strong faith was the basic reason for his good attitude.

I will never forget when he asked his oncologist, "Will I live through the current LSU football season? It looks like they are going to have a very good team this year." He did not survive to the mid-point of the season.

The last day that I was with him, I took him outside in his wheelchair to sit in the sunshine for about an hour. When he was ready to go in he said, "I won't be feeling the sunshine again until the resurrection. You know the last two weeks have been interesting. This dying has been quite a learning experience. Thank you son!"

LESSON 21: Set attainable goals that make you stretch and enjoy life.

Television and other passive activities have taken away much of the good things that make life pleasurable. That is not to say that there isn't some good in television. But when we look at the increasingly unproductive lifestyles of many, it seems apparent that they are willing to watch life rather than live it. This probably accounts for a large measure of the obesity experienced in this country.

Our generation has been told repeatedly, "If you want to be someplace different at this time next year, you have to start doing something different today." That is the same as saying that we need attainable goals.

Without goals we are like a ship adrift with the current. We don't know where we are going or why. Or we may just be content to let others dictate our direction. With goals, we have a target to shoot for, a destination to be reached, and a height to be attained.

Some experience the benefits of a goal when they begin to plan a periodic vacation. At first they are unclear on what it is they wish to do or where to go. They may even elect to stay home and accomplish some much needed gardening or preventative maintenance. Once the goal has been identified and established, our mind and hearts leap into action. We begin to strategize and plan how to best reach our goal. All of this infuses us with energy. We may even become productive in other areas.

It has been said that when challenged with an attainable goal, some people experience a high. They may say that food tastes better, they are sleeping better, they tend to smile more, they are more engaged, and often happier.

Baby boomers are beginning to establish goals, targets, destinations that will impact the world profoundly over the next twenty years. But, they will make sure that they are attainable goals. They will accomplish much. Some will try to cure cancer. Others will seek to beautify their lawn. Some will want to travel to the ends of the earth and converse with their fellowman. Others will want to ex-

pand their knowledge of a totally different field than that which oc-
cupied their career. All will benefit from setting attainable goals and
they will stretch and enjoy life.

* * *

Over the years there have been so many people that I have learned
from. One of the overriding things that I have learned is this: in
spite of sometimes difficult or desperate circumstances or even financial disaster, the boomers I have the greatest respect and admi-
ration for are the ones who never gave up and who never lost their
integrity while coping magnificently. They refused to look for
scapegoats nor did they attempt to shift blame for their situation
onto others. They took responsibility and looked for solutions.
They viewed even misfortune as just another experience to learn
from on the playing field we call life.

The satirical sense of humor of many baby boomers is legendary. With all the pending disaster hanging over our heads most of
our lives, it has been necessary to develop a sense of humor to
keep perspective on ever more disturbing, perplexing, and unfa-
thomable events.

This book has been about one baby boomer's quest for a meaningful, rewarding retirement with some resources available to allow freedom of choice. But the more I got into it, I realized that it
was really about learning to be a better person. It is about learning
how to cope with life's uncertainties. It is about being open-
minded, inquisitive, and curious about the things that mean the
most to us. It is also about finding ways to protect and grow, at
least to some extent, the resources we have available individually.
We must treat those resources as a trust and make every effort not
to squander them.

All in all, I am glad that my ex-financial planner is still my
friend. I still don't regret having fired him. The truth is, what I
viewed as his failure I now recognize was actually my own. I
failed to be personally involved and responsible for my assets. I
failed to make myself knowledgeable and then failed to establish
reasonable goals based on the way money actually works.

Achieving balance with respect to acquiring and managing financial wealth can bring enormous benefits. Happiness, peace of mind, and contentment have great value and they are not dependent upon great financial wealth.

J. Paul Getty, regarded as the richest man on earth during his lifetime said, "Happiness does not depend upon how much money you have. Instead, great wealth can cause great unhappiness." (Check out www.google.com for J. Paul Getty and you will see a listing of many of his quotes.) Late in life he sadly admitted, "I hate to be a failure. I hate and regret the failure of my marriages. I would gladly give all my millions for just one lasting marital success."

In contrast to J. Paul Getty, my father enjoyed a marriage of fifty-three years. He was a man who lived simply within his means and enjoyed a life of contentment in spite of any hardships he had to endure. He loved and cared for his four sons, leaving them not only a small estate but a legacy of integrity and honesty. I will always remember my father's common sense when it came to managing money and not allowing it to manage him.

After all these years of exploration, education, trial and error, success and failure, what conclusions must a humbled baby boomer arrive at?

There is no absolute expert when it comes to investment strategies. There is some risk associated with every program.

There is more information available through the Internet than anytime in history. Use it to become educated but test every recommendation. "Backtest" against proven benchmarks just like the world's most renowned investors.

Each investor seeking to protect and/or enlarge his or her potential retirement must be involved personally at least to some degree and not just leave matters in the hands of a financial advisor or planner. Plan, be involved and be proactive regarding retirement issues.

And I now know that whatever assets I have, they must be managed and placed in the best, safest places where they can grow. I must utilize those assets wisely for my family, my future, and any charitable purposes that I may identify. As I continue to strive for balance, I will manage my PRA with a purpose. Although unforeseen events will impact me, I will do my best to wisely steward the financial resources I have. I will look for ways to share what wealth I have by expanding my volunteer service and helping others where possible. Then I will be well on the way to realizing the kind of purposeful and rewarding retirement that brings happiness.

Epilogue
Reflections

Looking back on the past half century plus, lessons that were once fuzzy now seem crystal clear. Life is short and it is filled with challenges. I have faced many challenges and tests in my life. I have often failed. As I reflect on the decisions I made I am often simply amazed. The errors are glaring and my family and I suffered the consequences.

Regret over decisions I made and the bitterness caused by those decisions at times were almost too much to bear. On several occasions I almost let those feelings ruin me.

The turning point came for me when I confessed to myself that I could not blame anyone but myself for those poor decisions. At times adversaries used the leverage I provided to make matters worse. But the real culprit was me. When I honestly came to that realization, I immediately began to move forward putting the past behind.

The simple lesson I learned is that the only one we can really do anything about is ourselves. When we humbly acknowledge our own weaknesses, face them head on, and then make changes in the way we react or respond, we are bound to experience relief and happiness.

The twenty-one lessons contained herein have provided the lifeline for me as I faced the challenges of life and managing my own financial resources. In most cases those lessons are founded on eternal principles that are well expressed in the best book on living and managing money—the Holy Bible. But they will be like frozen treats unless we open the book, read these principles, and allow them to thaw as we meditate and permit them to settle into our hearts.

The lessons I learned have convinced me that having a balanced perspective regarding money is healthy. In most cases it is so difficult to acquire but very easy to squander or lose. Outside forces, unscrupulous individuals, and just time and unforeseen occurrence can rob us although we may make the best of decisions.

The truth is, making lots of money is not the source of true or lasting happiness. Giving of yourself to do something meaningful for others and doing it from the heart is what really counts. If you wish to have enduring happiness and contentment during your retirement years, it is worth the price.

Many years ago a dear friend of mine began to meet the challenge of managing money. He worked diligently, invested wisely, but never had making enormous amounts of money as his goal in life. Instead, he and his wife went into missionary work in the Philippines. After the birth of their two sons, they returned to the United States but continued to put spiritual things first in their lives. Their two sons are grown and now are busy in volunteer service following their parents' footsteps.

This couple later had the privilege of working to spiritually enrich others throughout Mexico. Now, in their later years, they are enjoying the challenges, excitement, and rewards of helping people in East Asia. On a recent trip to Asia I visited this couple. What a confirmation of all the lessons I had learned! This is a couple who have exemplified all the lessons contained herein.

After all these years, I have never met a couple more contented with their lives, more devoted to one another and more determined to remain busy helping other people. Even though advancing in years, this couple is more positive and more excited about the future than almost any retired couple I have ever met.

An amazing fact is that this couple, although never financially wealthy, has been self-sufficient. They have managed their resources by keeping their lives simple. They carefully invested what resources they had and stayed true to their commitment to living within their means.

Yet, they have never felt deprived. They have lived a good life. They eat well, are nicely clothed, and their modest three-bedroom, two-bath apartment allows for a small guestroom and an office.

They have traveled the world many times over. Their life together is filled with good friends and associates around the globe. They are welcomed wherever they go—not because they have great monetary wealth. No—they are welcomed because they have the greatest wealth of all—huge, giving hearts and true love for their fellow man. Their love for God and neighbor is evident in all they do. The fact is I view them as some of the richest people I know.

Managing money is just one of the challenges facing us short-lived humans. However, it can provide us some relief or it can be a life-long source of stress and pressure. There is a cost attached to all of our decisions. Which will it be for you?

My greatest desire in writing *Fire Your Financial Planner* has been to provide you with a stepping-stone to a happier retirement. However elusive, it is there. Whether it involves changing your approach to managing money or adjusting your attitude, it is within your reach. As the famous poet Robert Browning wrote: "Ah, but a man's reach should exceed his grasp. Or what's a heaven for?"

Appendix A
Confidential Estate Information Worksheet

	Investor	Spouse	Joint Assets
Real Estate			
Present Home	$_____	$_____	$_____
Other Real Estate	$_____	$_____	$_____
Vacation Home	$_____	$_____	$_____
Vehicles			
Cars	$_____	$_____	$_____
Boats	$_____	$_____	$_____
Motor Home	$_____	$_____	$_____
Investments			
Money Market	$_____	$_____	$_____
CDs	$_____	$_____	$_____
Stocks	$_____	$_____	$_____
Bonds	$_____	$_____	$_____
Mutual Funds	$_____	$_____	$_____
Commoditys	$_____	$_____	$_____
IRA,401(k),457,403(b)	$_____	$_____	$_____
Cash Accounts			
Checking	$_____	$_____	$_____
Savings	$_____	$_____	$_____
Insurance			
Life Insurance	$_____	$_____	$_____
Annuities	$_____	$_____	$_____

Miscellaneous

Personal Property	$_____	$_____	$_____
Household Goods	$_____	$_____	$_____
Business Interests	$_____	$_____	$_____
Collectible Loans	$_____	$_____	$_____
Legacy	$_____	$_____	$_____

GROSS ESTATE $_____ $_____ $_____

LIABILITIES $_____ $_____ $_____

NET ESTATE $_____ $_____ $_____

Name _____

Date _____/____/_____

(you may copy this form)

Appendix B
The Rule of 72

You need to know the Rule of 72! Einstein said that the Rule of 72 and the power of compounding of interest was the "greatest mathematical discovery of all time." The Rule of 72 tells you how long it will take for your money to double, and it's easy to calculate. Simply divide 72 by the percentage of return that you get on your savings or investments.

Example: You have a savings account with $10,000 in it. The bank pays 3 percent interest, so 72 divided by 3 is 24. It will take 24 years for your $10,000 to double to $20,000.

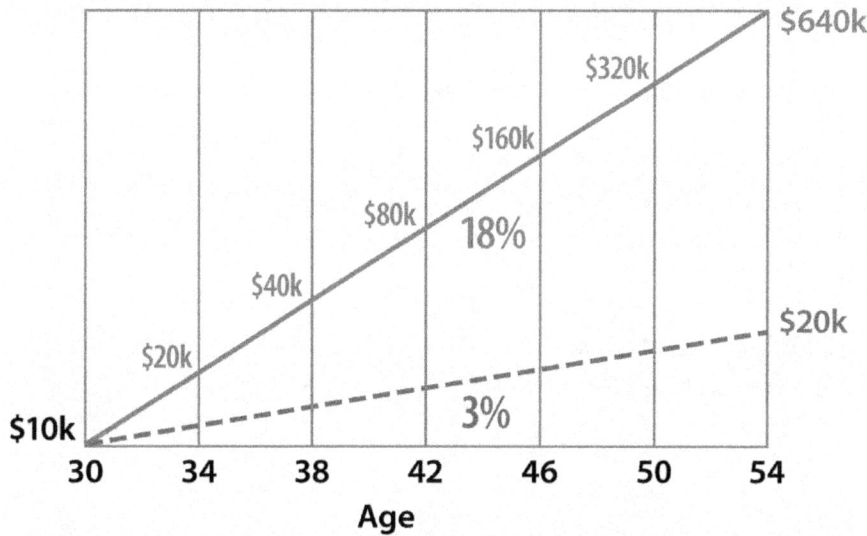

------- : A return of 3 percent would generate a doubling of the $10,000 to $20,000 over a 24-year period.

——————— : A return of 18 percent instead of 3 percent on the same $10,000 would grow to $640,000 over the same 24 years.

How Long Will It Take for Your Savings to Double?

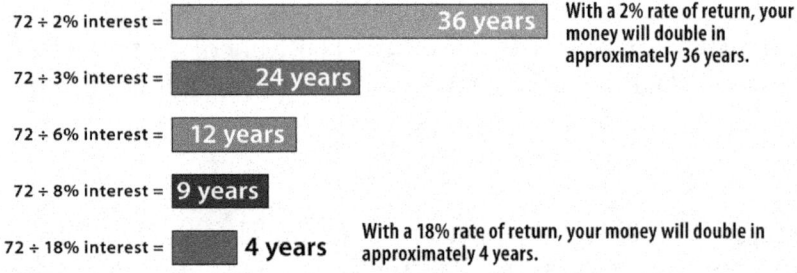

72 ÷ 2% interest = 36 years — With a 2% rate of return, your money will double in approximately 36 years.

72 ÷ 3% interest = 24 years

72 ÷ 6% interest = 12 years

72 ÷ 8% interest = 9 years

72 ÷ 18% interest = 4 years — With a 18% rate of return, your money will double in approximately 4 years.

Investment Comparisons

Investment Category	Rate of Return	Number of years to double
Money Market Account*	3.16%	22.7
1-Year Certificate of Deposit*	4.83%	14.9
5-Year Certificate of Deposit*	4.69%	15.35
Mutual Fund 10-Year Average**	6.97%	10.32

* Bankrate.com, 4-25-06
**Morningstar, 3-31-06

Appendix C
Types of Mortgages

Let's talk about different kinds of mortgage loans and, in the next Appendix, the confusing subject of amortization. As stated earlier, there are numerous options among which you may find just the right mortgage for you. Due to space constraints I can't list all of the many types of mortgage loans, but will focus on some of the more popular options.

Reverse Mortgage
In 1989, federally insured reverse mortgages became a viable option for seniors. The senior citizen organization AARP was instrumental in getting federal legislation passed to insure reverse mortgages.

This can be the right strategy for many seniors. Also called home equity conversion loans, reverse mortgages enable elderly homeowners to tap into their equity without selling their home. The lender pays out money based on the equity accrued in the home; the borrower receives a lump sum, a monthly payment, or a line of credit. Repayment is not necessary until the borrower sells the property, moves into a retirement community, or passes away. When the home is sold or no longer used as a primary residence, the borrower or his estate must repay the cash received from the reverse mortgage plus interest and other finance charges.

Most reverse mortgages require you be at least sixty-two years of age, have a low or zero balance owed against your home, and maintain the property as your principal residence. Reverse mortgages are ideal for homeowners who are retired or no longer working and need to supplement their income. Interest rates can be fixed or adjustable and the money is nontaxable and does not interfere with Social Security or Medicare benefits. Your lender cannot take property away if you outlive your loan, nor can you be forced to sell your home to pay off your loan, even if the loan balance grows to exceed property value.

It is important to note that this is a nonrecourse loan. With today's boomer generation defying all odds and living longer than previous generations, it is entirely possible that the accumulating interest could push the total debt above your home's value. However, that difference is paid by insurance built into the loan. Being a nonrecourse loan, no other part of your estate is ever at risk.

Another important feature to ask your financial planner about is that the proceeds are generally not subject to taxation. Ask which method of accepting the proceeds is best for your situation. You may receive proceeds in three ways:

- As a credit line (except in Texas), with either a fixed limit or a limit whose balance will increase each year equal to the interest rate you are charged.
- In a lump-sum cash payment.
- In monthly payments for a specified number of years or as long as you live in your home.

For more information on reverse mortgages, check out: www.aarp.org/money/revmort/.

Mortgage Freedom Loan
A different strategy that is gaining acceptance is promoted by Transcontinental Lending Group of Florida. They have developed a product called the mortgage freedom loan, which allows consumers to pay off their home mortgage in record time while not changing their payments or surrendering the powerful equity in their home.

About the mortgage freedom loan, it's been said it was created to assist borrowers who wished to accelerate their principal payments and do so as painlessly as possible. Just think how this could change the way Americans pay for their homes. They could capture the benefit of their money sitting in a checking account. The homeowner would get the benefit rather than the bank.

The following information was in an article dated 11/29/2007 by Carolyn Bigda, Money Magazine writer-reporter. This is representative of the many news reports as innovative, new mortgage alternatives become more widely known.

(Money Magazine) Question: (a reader asked this question) "I've heard that American lenders are now offering something called an offset mortgage, which is popular in the U.K. Do you think this is a good deal?"

Answer: "It depends. Here's how it works in Britain. You get a mortgage linked to a non-interest-bearing savings account whose deposits "offset" your loan balance. So if you owe $200,000 on your home but have $50,000 on deposit, the bank calculates your monthly interest as if you borrowed only $150,000. The bank gets its back scratched by getting to use your deposit interest-free. You pay off your mortgage faster because more of your monthly payment is applied to principal - and you can get your hands on your savings any old time. Because this deal would give you an extra weensy tax break under U.S. law, however, no offset mortgages are allowed here. But two U.S. companies - CMG Financial Services and Macquarie Mortgages USA - have introduced a version that passes muster with the IRS. You take out an adjustable-rate mortgage and deposit your paycheck into the mortgage account. Doing that gives you an offset on the principal, which lowers your interest. The arrangement could be useful if you receive big bonuses; you'll be reducing your interest until you use the money. But here's the real benefit: If you manage not to spend all your pay, you cut your costs. Say you save 5 percent of take-home pay of a gross income of $150,000 - about $460 a month. On a $300,000 7 percent mortgage, you'd slash your interest by $197,300 and be paid off in only 18 years - and you'd still have the money you saved. But if you spend more than you put in, the difference adds to your loan balance."

With the mortgage freedom loan, you direct-deposit your entire paycheck into your mortgage, instead of your checking account. This immediately reduces your principal balance. Since interest is based on your daily balance, you start saving interest immediately compared to traditional loans.

You pay all of your expenses out of your mortgage, just like you would a traditional bank account—using unlimited checks, free ATM/debit card, and free online bill-pay that comes with the account. Until you need the money, though, it is in your mortgage in the form of a lower principal balance, saving you 5 percent to 6 percent or more in mortgage interest, instead of earning 1 to 2 percent in a bank account. Less interest means that more of your take-home pay goes towards principal, and you pay off sooner. This is accomplished with no change in spending habits.

Take note of this caveat. This loan is not for individuals who do not have a plan to be debt-free. It is not for an individual who cannot control his finances. It is only allowed for individuals with an unblemished credit history and good credit scores.

In the case of a thirty-year fixed-rate loan, a borrower might also be able to obtain a home equity line of credit up to 90% or higher. Sometimes this ability might lead to difficulty down the road, even in a very conventional loan. Easy cash is tempting. How many times a month do you receive notices that your credit is approved by yet another credit card institution? You have two choices. You can either throw it in the trash or you can accept additional credit and open yourself up to more easy debt. Clearly, discretion is needed anytime you are dealing with how you use your creditworthiness.

Skip Wiley, the president of Transcontinental Lending Group, said in an interview on May 3, 2007, "Just as you would not give alcohol to an alcoholic, you don't give money to people who can't handle it." The mortgage freedom loan is for individuals who are seeking a financial transformation. It is for the financially prudent. Home equity represents a major portion of personal net worth for most boomers. It is essential that we are prudent in this matter, and that's why this option is worth investigating.

To learn all the potential benefits and parameters of this loan, you can go to several Web sites that also include calculators to help you determine if this loan is right for you (for more information see www.123smartmortgage.com or www.tlgmortgagerevolution.com.).

Even if interest rates go up, the numbers indicate there may still be substantial benefit from implementing this strategy. The Transcontinental Lending Group Web site states, "Our goal is to educate consumers, give them hope, encouragement, and a plan to change their financial destiny through a debt-free lifestyle."

Fixed-Rate Mortgage

With a fixed-rate mortgage, you know exactly what your principal and interest payment will be each month for the life of your loan. It won't change because your interest rate doesn't change. The taxes and insurance component of your payment towards escrow can change (and probably will), if your taxes and insurance change; unfortunately, there's no way to lock those in. If interest rates go up, you're protected with a fixed-rate mortgage. But you won't benefit if rates go down, although you can always take advantage of falling rates by refinancing. The fixed-rate loan can be for a period of thirty years (360 months) or fifteen years (180 months). The fifteen-year option can be for you if you want to minimize the amount of interest that you pay and reduce your balance quickly. All payments on these loans stay fixed at the original interest rate. Fixed rate mortgages might be right for you if you...

- Want the security of a fixed principal and interest payment.
- Think that interest rates will go up.
- Are on a fixed or limited budget.

Adjustable-Rate Mortgage (ARM)

Compared to fixed-rate mortgages, adjustable-rate mortgages (ARMs) offer a lower interest rate to start, so your monthly payments are generally lower. But the interest rate moves up and down with the market based on an index. Some of the more common indices include US Treasury bills, the Cost of Funds Index (COFI), and the London Interbank Offered Rate (LIBOR). Most ARMs have an initial fixed-rate period during which the interest rate doesn't change, followed by the rest of the loan's lifetime period in which the rate is adjusted at predetermined intervals. Many ARMs have caps that limit how much your interest rate can change per period, as well as for the life of the loan. Also be aware that there are some very low rates for ARMs that start out with discounted rates. These discounted rates are below the market rate and will definitely go up at the first adjustment period. Adjustable rate mortgages might be right for you if you:

- Want more property than you can qualify for now with a fixed rate.
- Are confident your income will increase or rates will not go up much.
- Plan on selling or refinancing within seven years of buying your home.

Jumbo Mortgages

Jumbo mortgages, or nonconforming loans, exceed the loan limits set by the two publicly chartered corporations (Fannie Mae and Freddie Mac) that buy mortgage loans from lenders. The 2005 single-family loan limit is $359,650. If you need to borrow more than that amount, you need a jumbo mortgage. These jumbo mortgages typically have a higher interest rate than conforming mortgages.

FHA Loans

The Federal Housing Administration (FHA) provides a loan-guarantee program instead of the standard private mortgage insurance (PMI), so qualified borrowers can get a mortgage loan with a down payment as low as 3 percent. The FHA doesn't make the loan, but rather they guarantee the loan, thus minimizing the lender's financial risk. FHA loans usually offer fairly liberal qualifying criteria compared to Fannie Mae and Freddie Mac and involve small down payments. They offer both fixed and adjustable loans.

Construction Loans

Construction loans are used to finance the building of a new home, rather than purchase an existing home. They are usually variable-rate loans that have interest-only payments during the construction phase. Draws to pay the builders are scheduled based on the stages of construction. Many construction loans are construction-to-permanent, which means that when construction is complete, the loan is converted to a normal mortgage. This has the advantage of a single loan with one closing.

Interest-Only Loans

There are a number of reasons that informed homeowners might choose an interest-only loan. For example, you may know that you will be in your current home no more than three to five years. That would be the case with some who are subject to job relocation from time to time. With a normally amortized loan, you would re-alize little reduction of principle in that period of time compared to the savings that you could incur in an interest-only loan. This could free up monies for other purposes: paying credit card debt, pur-chasing a vehicle, even college tuition; some use the savings to wisely invest those funds into an investment strategy that offers more than average returns.

You might choose an interest-only loan for flexibility in man-aging mortgage interest payments to maximize tax advantages, or to take advantage of lower initial interest rates and payments asso-ciated with monthly adjustable-rate mortgages. In this case the bor-rower would need to be comfortable with frequent payment fluctuations due to changing interest rates. Or it could be that you:

- Wish to buy as much house as possible.
- Plan to own the home for five years or less.
- Believe interest rates are likely to fall.
- Want the lowest possible payments.
- Have an unsteady income and need flexible payment options.

Power Option Loan

This mortgage product offers consumers the opportunity and flexi-bility to strategically manage their cash flow by utilizing four monthly payment options. With the power option loan you have the option to select the payment that best suits your financial situa-tion every month. It gives you control over your loan payment. The options are:

Option One: a fifteen-year fully amortizing payment.

Option Two: a thirty- year fully amortizing payment.

Option Three: an interest-only payment that allows you to take full advantage of the potential tax savings from a thirty-year mortgage while investing or utilizing the principal portion for retirement planning, college planning, debt consolidation, or any number of other needs that may arise.

Option Four: a minimum monthly payment option has a lower initial interest rate than the other three options for the first month of the loan. The initial interest and subsequent repayment rates depend on the investor you choose, credit, income and other market factors. This option not only maximizes cash flow, giving you more cash each month for other expenses, but also defers payment of interest on your loan. This may allow you greater flexibility in managing your deductions. Use of this option (in making only the minimum payment due each month) will result in negative amortization on your loan. (Note: Always consult your tax advisor relative to the right option for you. Option Four could result in deferred interest. This amount would be added to your loan balance.)

Appendix D
Amortization

How does amortization work? In the following example you will be shown the first five years of a typical thirty-year amortization schedule. You are shown five years because statistics in recent years say that most homeowners change their mortgage within five years. Some of the reasons for this include: moving to a larger home, downsizing, changing jobs, divorce, or just wanting a newer home with the latest gadgets.

The example assumes a thirty-year, fixed-rate loan at a 7 percent rate of interest. In this case, on the left side of the chart there is a regular payment schedule. The principal amount of the loan at closing is $150,000. The total payments in this example—if the loan is paid out over the entire thirty-year amortization—is $359,263.35. The total interest paid over that period is $209,263.35.

When you look at the right side of the chart, you will see the extra payment schedule. In this case, the assumption is made that you will make one additional monthly payment in June of each year. In doing so, your total payments over the course of the thirty-year loan would drop to $308,367.62. Your total interest paid over that period would be $159,296.64.

You should now begin to understand why it is important to have at least a rudimentary understanding of an amortization schedule. Notice that at the end of five years, in this example, you would still have a principal balance of $141,370.68. So on average over the first five years, you would have only $143.82 per month out of your $997.95 payment applied to principle. That is because a normally amortized loan is front-end loaded for interest. It is not until over twenty years or 240 months that the interest portion drops under $500 per month.

Regular Payment Schedule			Extra Payment Schedule		
Period	Monthly Payment	Interest Paid	Balance	Monthly Payment	Interest Paid	Balance
Jul-07			150,000.00			150,000.00
Aug-07	997.95	875.00	149,877.05	997.95	875.00	149,877.05
Sep-07	997.95	874.28	149,753.38	997.95	874.28	149,753.38
Oct-07	997.95	873.56	149,628.98	997.95	873.56	149,628.98
Nov-07	997.95	872.84	149,503.86	997.95	872.84	149,503.86
Dec-07	997.95	872.11	149,378.02	997.95	872.11	149,378.02
Jan-08	997.95	871.37	149,251.44	997.95	871.37	149,251.44
Feb-08	997.95	870.63	149,124.11	997.95	870.63	149,124.11
Mar-08	997.95	869.89	148,996.05	997.95	869.89	148,996.05
Apr-08	997.95	869.14	148,867.24	997.95	869.14	148,867.24
May-08	997.95	868.39	148,737.68	997.95	868.39	148,737.68
Jun-08	997.95	867.64	148,607.36	1,995.90	861.82	147,603.59
Jul-08	997.95	866.88	148,476.29	997.95	861.02	147,466.66
Aug-08	997.95	866.11	148,344.44	997.95	860.22	147,328.93
Sep-08	997.95	865.34	148,211.83	997.95	859.42	147,190.39
Oct-08	997.95	864.57	148,078.45	997.95	858.61	147,051.05
Nov-08	997.95	863.79	147,944.28	997.95	857.80	146,910.89
Dec-08	997.95	863.01	147,809.34	997.95	856.98	146,769.92
Jan-09	997.95	862.22	147,673.61	997.95	856.16	146,628.12
Feb-09	997.95	861.43	147,537.08	997.95	855.33	146,485.50
Mar-09	997.95	860.63	147,399.76	997.95	854.50	146,342.05
Apr-09	997.95	859.83	147,261.64	997.95	853.66	146,197.75
May-09	997.95	859.03	147,122.71	997.95	852.82	146,052.62
Jun-09	997.95	858.22	146,982.97	1,995.90	846.15	144,902.87
Jul-09	997.95	857.40	146,842.42	997.95	845.27	144,750.18
Aug-09	997.95	856.58	146,701.05	997.95	844.38	144,596.60
Sep-09	997.95	855.76	146,558.85	997.95	843.48	144,442.13
Oct-09	997.95	854.93	146,415.82	997.95	842.58	144,286.76
Nov-09	997.95	854.09	146,271.96	997.95	841.67	144,130.47
Dec-09	997.95	853.25	146,127.26	997.95	840.76	143,973.28
Jan-10	997.95	852.41	145,981.72	997.95	839.84	143,815.17
Feb-10	997.95	851.56	145,835.32	997.95	838.92	143,656.14
Mar-10	997.95	850.71	145,688.08	997.95	837.99	143,496.18
Apr-10	997.95	849.85	145,539.97	997.95	837.06	143,335.29
May-10	997.95	848.98	145,391.00	997.95	836.12	143,173.46
Jun-10	997.95	848.11	145,241.16	1,995.90	829.36	142,006.91
Jul-10	997.95	847.24	145,090.44	997.95	828.37	141,837.33
Aug-10	997.95	846.36	144,938.85	997.95	827.38	141,666.76
Sep-10	997.95	845.48	144,786.37	997.95	826.39	141,495.20
Oct-10	997.95	844.59	144,633.01	997.95	825.39	141,322.63
Nov-10	997.95	843.69	144,478.75	997.95	824.38	141,149.06

Dec-10	997.95	842.79	144,323.59	997.95	823.37	140,974.48
Jan-11	997.95	841.89	144,167.52	997.95	822.35	140,798.87
Feb-11	997.95	840.98	144,010.54	997.95	821.33	140,622.25
Mar-11	997.95	840.06	143,852.65	997.95	820.30	140,444.59
Apr-11	997.95	839.14	143,693.84	997.95	819.26	140,265.90
May-11	997.95	838.21	143,534.10	997.95	818.22	140,086.16
Jun-11	997.95	837.28	143,373.43	1,995.90	811.35	138,901.60
Jul-11	997.95	836.34	143,211.82	997.95	810.26	138,713.91
Aug-11	997.95	835.40	143,049.27	997.95	809.16	138,525.12
Sep-11	997.95	834.45	142,885.77	997.95	808.06	138,335.23
Oct-11	997.95	833.50	142,721.31	997.95	806.96	138,144.23
Nov-11	997.95	832.54	142,555.90	997.95	805.84	137,952.12
Dec-11	997.95	831.58	142,389.52	997.95	804.72	137,758.89
Jan-12	997.95	830.61	142,222.17	997.95	803.59	137,564.53
Feb-12	997.95	829.63	142,053.85	997.95	802.46	137,369.03
Mar-12	997.95	828.65	141,884.54	997.95	801.32	137,172.40
Apr-12	997.95	827.66	141,714.25	997.95	800.17	136,974.62
May-12	997.95	826.67	141,542.96	997.95	799.02	136,775.68
Jun-12	997.95	825.67	141,370.68	1,995.90	792.04	135,571.81

Appendix E
Things to Know About a 1031 Exchange

A 1031 exchange allows property owners to postpone taxes on the sale of investment property, provided that property is exchanged for like-kind investment property of an equal or greater value. The property may be vacant land, rental property, or property used for trade, business, or investment.

You should know about these things when contemplating an exchange:

Qualified Intermediary (QI)
The Internal Revenue Service requires that you use a QI to prepare the legal documents for your exchange. The QI must hold your money, so that you do not have access to it.

Property Use
Both your old and new property must qualify as investment or business use.

Related Party Exchanges
Special rules apply for exchanges between related persons. Non-recognition of gain is *denied* in an exchange if a taxpayer exchanges property with a related person, such as a spouse or lineal ancestors and descendants.

Reinvestment
In order to defer all of your capital gains tax, you must buy a new property equal to or higher in value than the one you are replacing.

Title Holding

You must purchase and take title to your new property exactly as you held your old property.

Forty-Five-Day Identification Period

You have forty-five days from the closing of your sale to list the properties you may want to purchase in your 1031. This must be delivered to the QI in writing on or before the forty-five-day deadline.

Completion of 1031

From the date of the sale, you have 180 days to close on the purchase of one or more properties from the forty-five-day identification list or until the due date of your tax return, whichever comes first.

Appendix F
Trusts

It is necessary for you to know about something called the federal estate tax exclusion. This is available when utilizing a trust. The exclusion is $2,000,000 per person. So in the case of a husband and wife, the total is $4,000,000. When your estate is passed on to your heirs, there will be no federal estate tax liability up to the amount of the exclusion. Most states follow the federal guidelines. Some states, however, only allow an exclusion of up to $1,000,000 per person.

The minimum federal tax applied to any funds not covered by this exclusion is 37.5 percent. That does not include anywhere from a 5.5 percent to 9.5 percent state estate tax that also applies to any funds not covered by the exclusion.

Single A Trust
This trust is appropriate for a single individual or for a married couple who own separate property and who do not own any joint property and would like a separate trust for each party.

Married A Trust
Appropriate for a husband and wife whose entire estate (including insurance) will definitely remain substantially less than one federal estate tax exclusion. Because of the potential impact of inflation on an estate, an AB trust may be best for a married couple, regardless of the estate size. Only one federal estate tax exclusion is available with this trust, so in effect you throw away the ability to use both federal estate tax exclusions. This trust is rarely recommended.

Married AB Trust

Appropriate for a husband and wife whose estate is less than and not expected to exceed the equivalent of two federal estate tax deductions.

Married ABC (Q-TIP) Trust

Appropriate for a husband and wife interested in preserving both federal estate tax exclusions and deferring the payment of estate taxes as long as possible when their estate exceeds or may exceed the equivalent of two federal estate tax exclusions. This trust includes Q-TIP and Q-DOT language and should not be selected when one or both parties is a resident/non-citizen of the US.

Unmarried AB Trust

Appropriate for unmarried couples, regardless of gender, who wish to have joint ownership of the assets in one trust.

Partner AA Trust

Appropriate for unmarried couples, regardless of gender, who wish to own their assets in separate trusts.

Single A Q-TIP Trust

Appropriate only for a husband or wife who prefer two separate trusts rather than a joint trust.

With the trusts listed above, you will also need the following documents:

- Pour-Over Will
- Living Will
- Durable Power of Attorney for Assets
- Durable Power of Attorney–Health Care (Advance Directive/Health Care Proxy)
- Nomination of Conservator
- Appointment of Guardian For Minor or Disabled Children
- Assignment of Furnishings and Personal Effects
- Trust Certification

- Letter of Instruction
- Transfer Letters, and
- Comprehensive Instruction and Forms for Estate Management

Additional estate-planning options include:

Alternate State B Trust Addition
This unique trust amendment to existing estate plan trusts is used when your state estate tax threshold is lower than the federal estate tax exclusion.

Asset Management Trust
An irrevocable trust designed to hold assets for a beneficiary with asset management problems. Also appropriate for special needs trust.

Beneficiary Trust
A trust designed to permit any of your beneficiaries to have control over the assets left to them while keeping those assets protected against the claims of creditors, divorcing spouses, and future estate taxes.

Bill of Sale
Transfers untitled assets into your living trust, such as sole proprietorship interests, collections, jewelry, farm equipment, business inventories, and valuable personal property.

Catastrophic Illness Trust
There are two types. The irrevocable CIT and the revocable Family CIT. If timely organized and funded, it can protect your estate from the cost of an illness or disability that may otherwise deplete your estate's assets.

Charitable Remainder Trust
A trust that is especially ideal for handling highly appreciated assets such as stock, real estate, or a family-owned business gives offspring the use of such assets during the Trustor's lifetime, then gifting assets upon the death of the Trustor to designated charities.

Family Limited Partnership
Designed to reduce the value of your taxable estate, provide maximum flexibility, and creditor protection while permitting you to retain control over your assets that are owned by the partnership. This is a legal entity consisting of a general partner and one or more limited partners. It can be used to protect assets from litigation and reduce or eliminate estate taxes and generation skipping taxes.

Insurance Preservation Trusts
A trust designed to keep life insurance out of your taxable estate to avoid consumption by taxes and to provide a relatively low-cost way to pay federal estate taxes. If your life insurance plus your net worth exceeds or may exceed the federal estate tax exclusion, this trust may be used to avoid unnecessary and otherwise avoidable estate taxes on life insurance.

Appendix G
Tips for Better Fuel Economy

Given the cost of gasoline, every budget can benefit from making the most of it. Here are some tips for better fuel economy from the US Department of Energy and the US Environmental Protection Agency.

Drive sensibly. Don't rapidly accelerate and brake. This can lower your gas mileage by 33 percent at highway speeds and by 5 percent around town.

Observe the speed limit. Gas mileage usually decreases rapidly at speeds above 60 mph. Each 5 mph you drive over 60 mph is like paying an additional 20 cents per gallon for gas.

Remove excess weight. Remove unnecessary items, heavy items from your trunk or cargo area. An extra 100 pounds in your vehicle could reduce your mpg by up to 2 percent. Remove roof racks if you aren't toting your bikes or kayaks around.

Avoid excessive idling.

Use cruise control on the highway to maintain constant speed, which, in most cases, saves gas.

Keep your engine properly tuned and check and replace air filters regularly.

Keep tires properly inflated, which can improve mileage by about 3 percent.

Drive a more efficient vehicle. The difference between a car that gets 20 mpg and one that gets 30 mpg amounts to $744 per year (assuming 15,000 miles of driving annually and a fuel cost of $2.97).

Appendix H
Recommended Reading

Andrew, Douglas R., *Missed Fortune* (Warner Books, Inc., 2004). Explodes all the common beliefs about personal investing and challenges readers on their most fundamental principles on how to build wealth.

Anthony, Mitch, *The New Retirementality* (Kaplan Publishing, 2006). A must-read guide for the baby boomer generation. This book is all about a new way of thinking that I strongly recommend.

Bible, The (particularly the book of Proverbs). "Happy is the man that findeth wisdom, And the man that getteth understanding. For the gaining of it is better than the gaining of silver, And the profit thereof than fine gold" (Proverbs 3:13–14)

Brock, Fred, *Retire On Less Than You Think* (Times Books, 2004). Fred Brock debunks the myths concocted by the mutual fund industry about retirement. He gives instead strategies and tools for achieving your personal retirement plans.

Colbert, David, *Eyewitness to Wall Street* (Broadway Books, 2001). David Colbert covers 400 years of history of Wall Street from Dutch New Amsterdam in the early 1600s to the year 2000. The focus here is on people, not numbers.

Edelman, Ric, *Ordinary People—Extraordinary Wealth* (Harper-Collins, 2002). One of the nation's best-known and most successful financial

advisors offers eight unconventional strategies for smart investing based on his survey of 5,000 of his most successful clients.

Edelman, Ric, *The New Rules Of Money* (HarperCollins, 2005).
Forget what you know about personal finance. The old rules no
longer apply. Ric Edelman's eighty-eight strategies, tailor-
made for today's economy, will show you how to achieve financial success.

Edelman, Ric, *The Truth About Money* (Harper Collins, 2003).
Real advice from one of America's most successful financial
advisors.

Rutner, Richard, *The Trouble With Mutual Funds* (Financial Press,
Inc., 2003).
Be warned. If you invest in mutual funds, this little book is
guaranteed to worry you. Get behind the scenes of the modern
mutual fund industry and discover the real reasons that mutual
funds perform so poorly.

St. John, Bonnie, *Money: Fall Down? Get Up!* (St. John Deane,
Inc., 2002).
The easiest, most inspirational and impactful book on money
ever written.

Appendix I

Resources: Featured Individuals, Companies, and Organizations

(The following information regarding these entities is reprinted here with their express consent.)

Ric Edelman, CFS, CMFC®, RFC®, CRC®, QFP, BCM, EIEIO
Ric Edelman is one of the nation's most acclaimed financial advisors. He and his firm have won more than sixty financial, business, community, and philanthropic awards, and his commitment to teaching consumers about personal finance has established him as one of the most popular financial professionals in America.
www.ricedelman.com

Transcontinental Lending Group
Founded in 1996 and run by its founder and longtime industry professional, Skip Wiley, TLG has been positioning itself in 2006–2007 to market its Freedom Mortgage Loan nationally. With its many branches and associates, TLG's goal is to reach each region of the country with this product over the next two years.
www.123smartmortgage.com
www.tlgmortgagerevolution.com
www.tlg.bz

FOLIOfn
FOLIOfn, Inc., is an innovative brokerage and investment solutions company serving individual investors, financial advisors, and financial institutions around the world. It offers its leading-edge

brokerage services on both a full-service basis and a technology-licensed basis. Through its wholly-owned, registered clearing broker-dealer subsidiary, FOLIOfn Investments, Inc. (member, NASD/SIPC), the company offers an integrated brokerage and technology platform featuring its patented, state-of-the-art folio trading capability, as well as execution, clearance, and settlement services. FOLIOfn was established in 1998 by Steven Wallman, a former commissioner of the Securities and Exchange Commission, who was widely recognized during his tenure as an investor advocate. The privately held company is headquartered in Vienna, Virginia.
www.foliofn.com

StockDiagnostics.com

Stock Diagnostics.com (SDX) believes that the health of any company is determined primarily by its cash flow. Portfolios are assembled based on the data extrapolated from quarterly and yearly reports of publicly traded companies. SDX looks at a number of proprietary algorithms that allow them to pick companies with good operational cash flow per share (OPS).
www.stockdiagnostics.com

TheRetirementSolution.com

The Retirement Solution Inc. presently sells and markets a proprietary "retirement solution," which consists of monthly subscription offerings to proprietary information that is provided by StockDiagnostics.com. The Retirement Solution, Inc., believes that it has a revolutionary solution to retirement because individuals have two ways in which to benefit. The first is that those with portfolios have exclusive access to superior investment information that is provided by StockDiagnostics. The second benefit is that individuals can augment or supplement their retirement income by selling subscriptions that enable them to earn residual income.
www.theretirementsolution.com

JGO Financial

JGO Financial is dedicated to empowering the individual investor

by providing the education and tools necessary to become educated about your retirement future through training, research tools, and industry newsletters. By providing simple, easy-to-understand information to its representatives, JGO Financial caters to the majority of people who want to learn more about investing. Online research tools allow you to learn at your own pace and develop a better sense of security about your investments. Now you can be directly involved in the growth of your retirement account.
www.jgofinancial.com

Global Equity Lending
Global Equity Lending is one of the nation's premier mortgage lenders/brokers, offering an ever-expanding portfolio of both residential and commercial products from some of the most respected companies in the industry.
www.globalequitylending.com

Investools
With more than a quarter of a million graduates, Investools is a leader in investor education. The curriculum teaches beginning and experienced investors alike how to evaluate markets and make smarter decisions about when, where, and how to invest.
www.investools.com

TD Ameritrade
Offering online trading, the goal is to give you the best available online trading tools and information to help you quickly enter orders and spot and track potential opportunities. Using a proprietary order-routing system that allows the company to dynamically distribute orders to multiple market centers, getting the fastest execution for your orders. With the TD Ameritrade 5-Second Guarantee, qualifying S&P 100® Internet equity market trades that take longer than 5 seconds to execute are commission-free! You also have have a wide choice of investment vehicles like stocks, options, and mutual funds to implement your unique trading strategy.
www.TDAMERITRADE.com

Scottrade
For more than twenty-five years, Scottrade has been a leader in the stock brokerage industry—in technology, customer service, and value. Today at Scottrade, investors have the stock trading tools and services they need to take control of their investing needs. Scottrade is proud to provide premium service and deeply discounted commissions to investors of all trading styles and plans to continue to exceed its customers' expectations by providing the best price, the best service, and the best technology.
www.scottrade.com

The Motley Fool
David and Tom Gardner—cofounders of The Motley Fool—bring you an investment service with an outstanding track record. The strategy is simple and powerfully rewarding: you receive two stock recommendations each month. Whether you have $250 to invest or tens of thousands of dollars, they claim their careful business research can help you beat the market soundly, en route to living a life without financial concern.
www.themotleyfool.com

National Association of Personal Financial Advisors
NAPFA, the National Association of Personal Financial Advisors, is the nation's leading organization dedicated to the advancement of fee-only comprehensive financial planning. Consumers and the media look to NAPFA for access to financial advisors who meet the highest standards for professional competency, comprehensive financial planning, and fee-only compensation.
www.NAPFA.com

Securities and Exchange Commission
The mission of the US Securities and Exchange Commission is to protect investors, maintain fair, orderly, and efficient markets, and facilitate capital formation. As more and more first-time investors turn to the markets to help secure their futures, pay for homes, and send children to college, the SEC's investor protection mission is more compelling than ever. And as our nation's securities exchanges mature into global for-profit competitors, there is even greater need for sound market regulation.
www.sec.gov

End Notes

1. Richard Lehmann, *"Retirement Realities,"* *Forbes*, 7 March 2006.
2. Mitch Anthony, *The New Retirementality* (New York: Kaplan Publishing, 2006).
3. William Kosoff, President, The Retirement Solution.com, 10 October 2006.
4. Scott Burns, "How the 401K system fails most people," MSN Money, http://moneycentral.msn.com/content/RetirementandWills/P90046.asp. Accessed on 5 September 2007.
5. Arianna Huffington, "Another Tale of Corporate Greed," Salon.com, 7 May 2002.
6. Huck Gutman, "Dishonesty, Greed and Hypocrisy in Corporate America," *The Statesman* (Calcutta, India), 14 July 2002.
7. Pentagon FCU press release, Associated Press, Alexandria, VA, 17 October 2005.
8. "Fannie Mae Settlement Disbursements Begin," Associated Press, 1 May 2007.
9. Ric Edelman, *Ordinary People—Extraordinary Wealth* (Collins, 2000).
10. Ibid.

Index

www.ingramcontent.com/pod-product-compliance
Lightning Source LLC
Chambersburg PA
CBHW051533170526
45165CB00002B/710